EACH DAY NEW YOU

69 MINDFUL RHYMES FOR DIFFICULT AND CHALLENGING TIMES

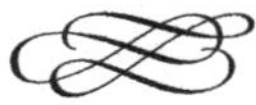

A-J PATERSON

CONTENTS

COPYRIGHT

Published in 2020 by miniteaching media

Each day New you

A-J Paterson 2020 © FIRST EDITION

miniteaching.com, contact info@miniteaching.com

ISBN

This is a work of creative nonfiction. Some parts have been fictionalised in varying degrees, for various purposes.

❀ Created with Vellum

ACKNOWLEDGMENTS

I would like to thank you for choosing my book on your journey to self-discovery. I hope you find it of value, whether your approach is for inspiration or to delve deeper into self-reflection.

I thank my parents and family, especially my partner and children whom I love dearly, for making my world a fun, supportive, encouraging and loving place to be.

I thank all those positive thinkers, speakers and authors for laying the foundations of living with meaning through their inspirational words and lives. Each positive humanitarian born to the world gives hope for others facing the difficulties and challenges of life.

INTRODUCTION

Welcome readers. Whether you have purchased "Each day New You", or received it as a gift, I can assure you that it will prove a great guide for seasoned self-help pilgrims and those who are just beginning their journey into self-help. Each day you will experience a new you!

The secret to "Each day New You", compared to other self-help books and journals, is in its minimal presentation. You will find straightforward, personal learning that is immediately delivered in memorable words through four distinct stages:

1. Learning a memorable rhyme to repeat as an affirmation in times of difficulty or challenge.
2. Contemplating a brief description which reinforces the rhyme's message.
3. Answering thought-provoking questions in preparation for using the rhyme in the day to come.
4. Exploring further self-discovery questions, inspiring you to take action throughout the following day, then reflecting on your experience at the day's end.

All four elements bring the rhyme's message into reality, through your day-to-day encounters and experiences. You cannot but make a change!

Advice for working through "Each day New you".

- The book does not have to be read in a linear, page-by-page fashion.
- You can search the contents and choose the area relevant to the problem you are experiencing right at this moment, and dive deep!
- Or choose a less urgent area of your life where you seek improvement.
- At other times you may choose to simply read the rhymes for inspiration!

"Each day New You" has been put together through many hours of thorough self-reflection, and helping others to achieve significant life changes. I have only committed tried-and-tested approaches to print and have prompted your full participation and reflection in the journal pages through insightful questions.

As you work through the journal, noticeable changes will begin to happen; your understanding of yourself will deepen and your view of the world will change for the better.

Enjoy your journey and I wish you great success,

A-J Paterson

ILLUSTRATIONS

The illustrations contained in this book are randomly, computer-generated mandalas using free online graphics generators.

The word "Mandala" comes from Sanskrit and means "disc". A mandala has a geometric pattern, shaped in a circular style. Older mandalas have a square shape with four "T" shaped gates containing a circle at the very centre.

The mandala style crosses many faiths. In Hinduism and Buddhism, it represents the universe and connection. It is also found in many Christian symbols such as those found in stained glass windows in the form of a halo, the Celtic and Rosy cross, Jesus Crown of Thorns, the rosary, the aureole circle of light, the oculi, and the labyrinths found on cathedral floors.

Many pilgrimages to Cathedrals, involve walking the labyrinth and praying or contemplating on the way to the centre, figuratively, the pilgrim is centring themselves.

RHYME I
STAND UPRIGHT

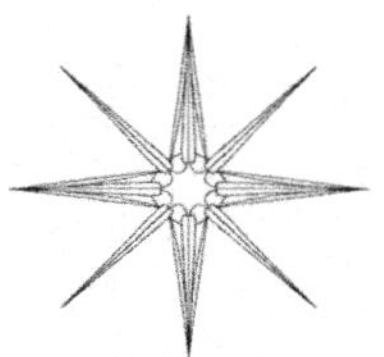

RHYME 1

STAND UPRIGHT

Head up and shoulders back,

---

be cheerful when you interact.

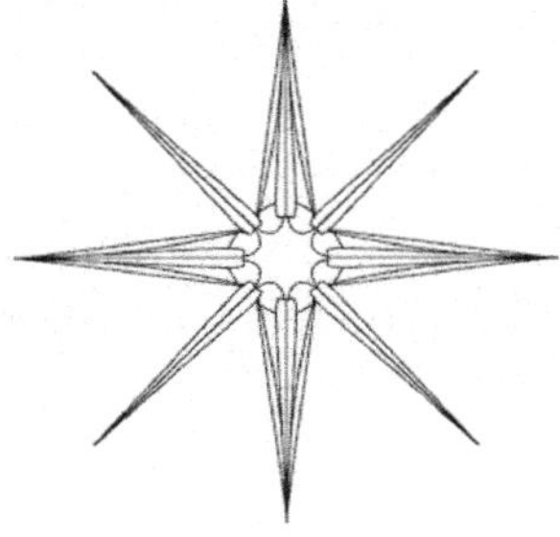

STAND UPRIGHT

Standing upright gives the impression of confidence even when you don't feel it.

This positive change of physical state will influence your thoughts for the better.

Embrace this habit: When you feel your worst, present your best.

PREPARATION FOR USING RHYME 1

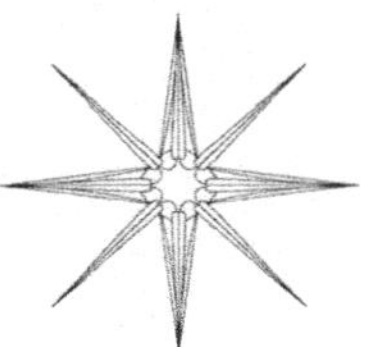

Are any thoughts or feelings holding me back from presenting myself in a confident and cheerful manner with others?

WHAT CONSCIOUS REMINDERS can I think of to assist me in maintaining an upright and positive state throughout the day?

WHAT POSSIBILITIES and opportunities can I foresee this week to consciously practice presenting myself in a more upright and cheerful way?

PUTTING RHYME 1 INTO ACTION

What did I personally experience from standing up straight and being more cheerful?

Did any noticeably positive reactions from others occur, or did I feel better in myself?

What reflections, from my experience or observing others, do I have about an upright and cheerful approach to life?

RHYME II
TAKE INITIATIVE

RHYME 2

TAKE INITIATIVE

You may delay but others will not,

---

strike whilst the iron's hot.

TAKE INITIATIVE

When opportunities present themselves,

---

be the first

---

to take the initiative.

PREPARATION FOR USING RHYME 2

What one thing do I need to take action on now before it slips from my grasp or is claimed by another?

WHAT FEELINGS or thoughts stop me from taking up opportunities when they present themselves?

WHAT DO I need to begin to do to embrace opportunities rather than watch others take them?

PUTTING RHYME 2 INTO ACTION

How can I be more conscious of taking opportunities as they appear today?

WHAT DID others do today to embrace an opportunity and what can I learn from them?

CAN I recall all the opportunities I noticed today and possible opportunities for tomorrow?

RHYME III
EXPECT CHALLENGE

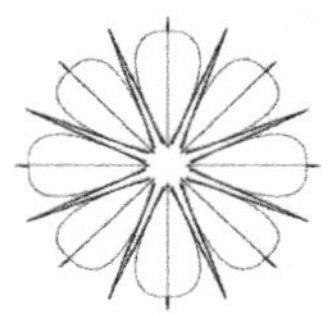

RHYME 3

EXPECT CHALLENGE

As you paddle life's stream amidst the flotsam and jetsam,

much that bumps into you isn't worth your attention.

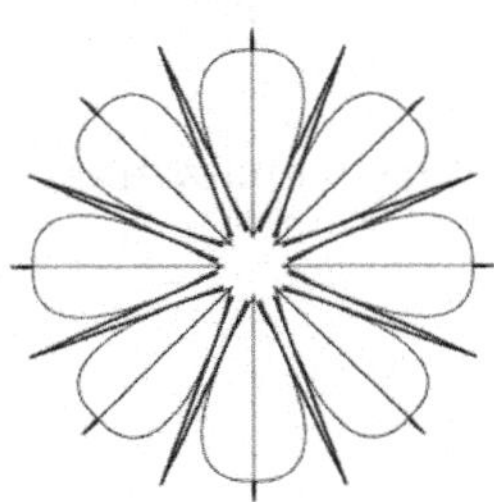

EXPECT CHALLENGE

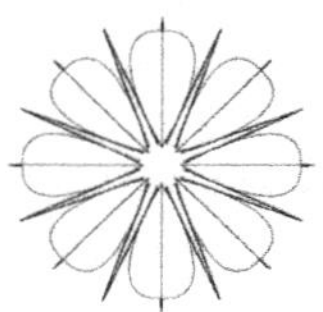

Most things that bother us have done no real damage;

---

if it hasn't happened,

---

it hasn't happened.

PREPARATION FOR USING RHYME 3

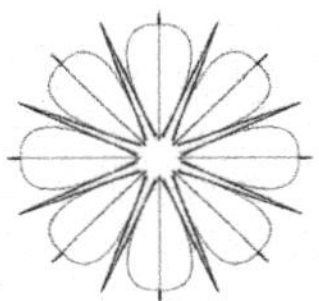

List some real challenges that bother me in my day-to-day life?

WHAT IMAGINED challenges make me anxious, slow me down, or halt me in my tracks?

WHAT POSITIVE STRATEGIES can I have prepared when I experience these challenges?

PUTTING RHYME 3 INTO ACTION

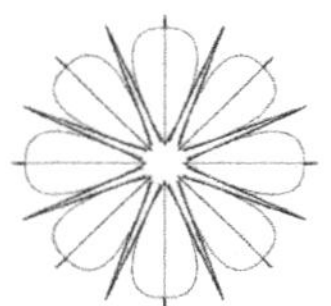

When a challenge arises, put it in perspective:
What is the worst that can happen to me?

OUT OF TEN, with one being the lowest and ten being the highest, how bothersome is this challenge in the scheme of other life events?

Is this challenge in my control and can I do something about it now?

Is this challenge out of my control and I need to draw on my resilience to accept it, ignore it, or seek outside support?

RHYME IV
READY… LAUNCH

RHYME 4

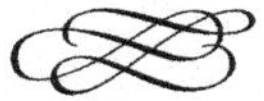

READY... LAUNCH

What's the one thing you can do right now,

to launch your idea off the ground.

READY… LAUNCH

Take one small action now towards the idea that is currently firing your thoughts.

It may lead to more compelling ideas and actions,

---

and take off!

PREPARATION FOR USING RHYME 4

When I have ideas flowing in my mind, I can explore them by:

- Writing them down
- Listing them
- Brainstorming
- Mind mapping
- Reading a related blog or internet article
- Watching a related YouTube topic with someone who has experience and advice in the field
- Contacting someone who has knowledge or experience in the area whom I can ask questions of

---

Now is the time to begin capturing my ideas and plan how I will explore them.

PUTTING RHYME 4 INTO ACTION

Prepare all my stationary or other tools ahead of time and remove ALL my known distractions.

Set a timer for 5 minutes.

Within that time, solidly work without interruption on writing, researching, contacting others or physically doing something towards my idea.

The 5-minute timer may lead to many more absorbing minutes after it has chimed.

Begin Now!

RHYME V
BE CONSTRUCTIVE

RHYME 5

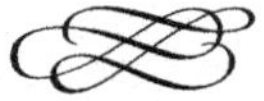

BE CONSTRUCTIVE

Don't criticise, complain, nor frown,

---

build an idea, don't tear it down.

BE CONSTRUCTIVE

We move towards a destination step-by-step;

---

we build a creation piece-by-piece.

On the flip-side, we cause harm by pulling down the ideas, dreams, personality and appearance of others.

PREPARATION FOR USING RHYME 5

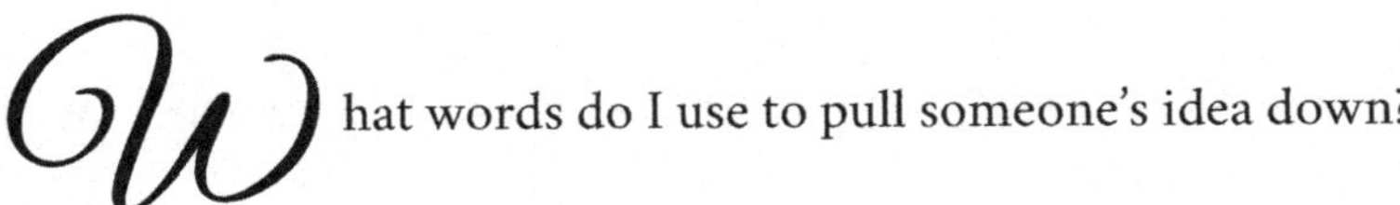

What words do I use to pull someone's idea down?

When I do this, how do I appear to them and what emotions do I project upon the unfortunate victim?

What feeling/s am I trying to experience from pulling down another's worth or ideas?

How can I experience this same feeling in a constructive way, rather than at the expense of another?

PUTTING RHYME 5 INTO ACTION

If I'm tempted to undermine another person, I will choose to:

- bite my tongue and just listen
- gather my thoughts with a deep breath, hold and let it out
- know I am more mature by not being a critic
- offer constructive support in a modest way

If I am being led into a habitual path of conversational gossip, I will consciously change the conversation from a person to an object or experience, that those in my company can relate to and are interested in.

WHAT ALTERNATE EVENTS or observations can I prepare to discuss that do not involve other people in a negative way?

RHYME VI
SHOW APPRECIATION

RHYME 6

SHOW APPRECIATION

Give simple, honest appreciation,

it's the personal glue that bonds affection.

SHOW APPRECIATION

As naturally social beings, our lives are enhanced by our relationships with others.

We build relationships by

---

appreciating the existence of one another.

PREPARATION FOR USING RHYME 6

The quickest way for me to isolate someone is to sensorily ignore them, i.e. no eye contact, headphones on, no recognition of their existence. The quickest way for me to validate another's existence is to:

- make eye contact and smile
- say 'Hi' when they first appear in the room
- laugh at a shared joke
- listen without interruption and nod my head in acknowledgement or agreement
- say the person's name in a warm way
- quietly sit nearby in their company
- comment on our shared environment, the weather or a shared interest

---

WHAT TECHNIQUES WORK naturally for my personality?

PUTTING RHYME 6 INTO ACTION

Acknowledgement Checklist

TODAY, have I made a connection every time someone has entered the room? Why or Why not?

WHAT SPECIFICALLY DID I use to make a connection?

- A smile
- Saying their name
- A nod
- Saying 'Hi'
- Asking how they are or casually chit-chatting about the immediate environment or weather.
- Quietly being in their presence.

RHYME VII
BE DECISIVE

RHYME 7

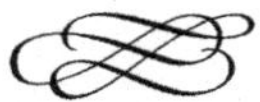

BE DECISIVE

Do, delegate, delay or ditch,

is how to deal with any hitch.

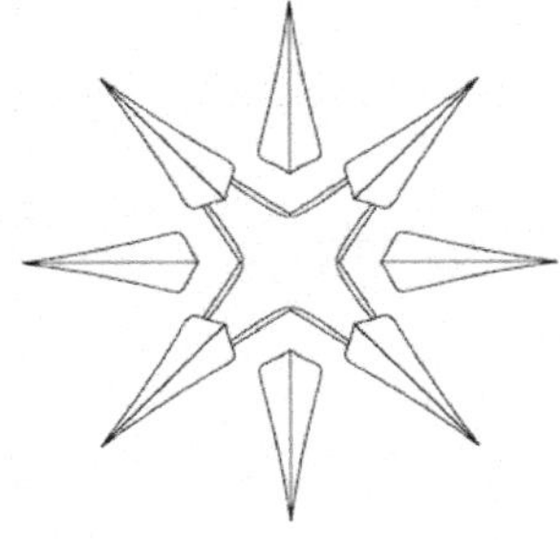

BE DECISIVE

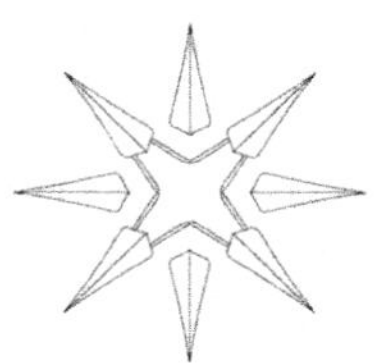

It is not mentally or physically healthy to control everything yourself and shows a lack of trust in others' capabilities.

Instead, improve others' potential and let them exercise their talents.

Discard 'busy work' as it has no value.

PREPARATION FOR USING RHYME 7

What are the strengths and weaknesses of the people around me?

MAKE a confidential note of their known abilities, talents, ambitions, personality traits and relationship skills, honestly and without favouritism.

SPLIT THE TASKS/CHORES/PROJECTS that need to be completed beside the following headings:

- DO what I need to complete as a priority.
- DELEGATE to the right person for the job.
- DELAY until a later date and then decide.
- DITCH it as it makes no impact of value.

PUTTING RHYME 7 INTO ACTION

I will always positively inspire others and seek their agreement before delegating a responsibility for a task.

It must be something that I would do myself if I could manage the time or admit that I don't have the skills for.

TODAY, I will delegate the following tasks to others and inspire their responsibility through praising their unique talents?

WHAT ARE the important tasks for me to complete today and what can I delay or discard?

RHYME VIII
PERSONABLY LEAD

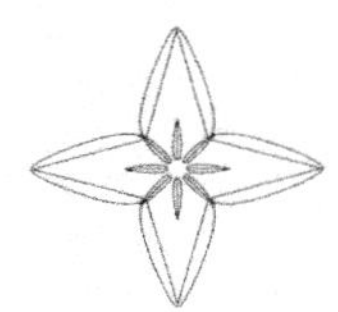

RHYME 8

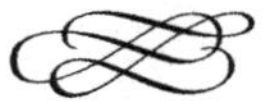

PERSONABLY LEAD

Through coaching, direction and delegation,

---

your team will reach their destination.

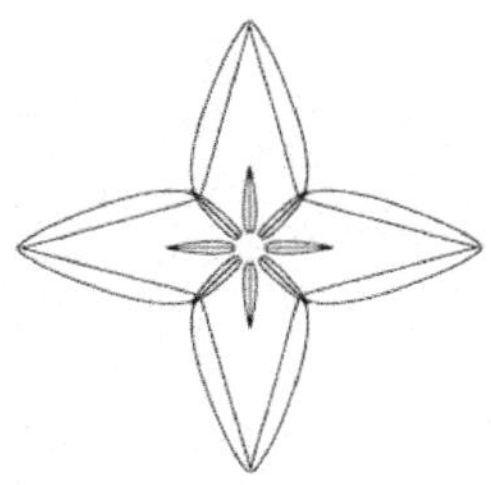

PERSONABLY LEAD

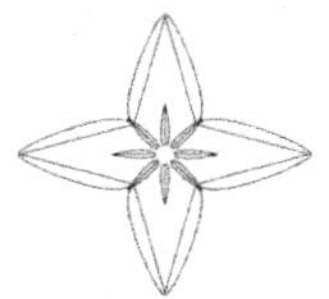

A Leader is the Shepherd of the flock they lead.

They enable the passion and commitment of those in their care, in business and daily life,

---

to achieve the greater good of their tenure.

PREPARATION FOR USING RHYME 8

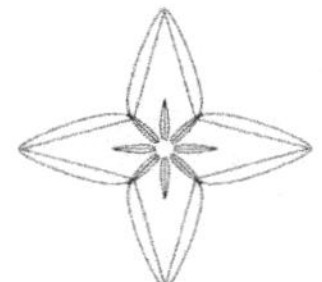

Who are the people I guide and lead in life through my deeper knowledge, care and experience?

WHO DO I direct more than others, knowing that my influence could shape them to be a future role-model too?

WHAT FORESEEN opportunities do I have this week to coach another to improve their experience and knowledge?

WHAT DO I need to improve in my leadership style? e.g. my confidence, personal relationships, less control and interference, respect for others, modesty, clarity in explanation.

PUTTING RHYME 8 INTO ACTION

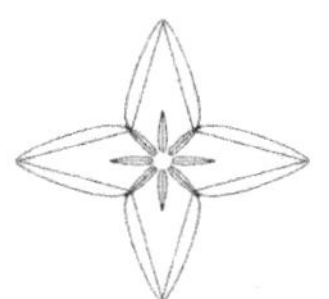

What were the opportunities for leadership I had today?

WHAT WERE the highlights or lowlights?

HOW DO I feel people responded to my lead today?

HOW COULD I improve my leadership approach or knowledge for next time?

RHYME IX
DEVELOP EFFECTIVELY

RHYME 9

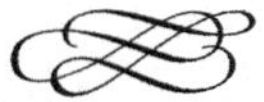

DEVELOP EFFECTIVELY

Create, improve, remove or accept,

---

are the only decisions in development.

DEVELOP EFFECTIVELY

The Developer keeps an objective eye on approaches that work and don't work,

---

is adaptable for the benefit of themselves, others,

---

and the success of day-to-day business.

PREPARATION FOR USING RHYME 9

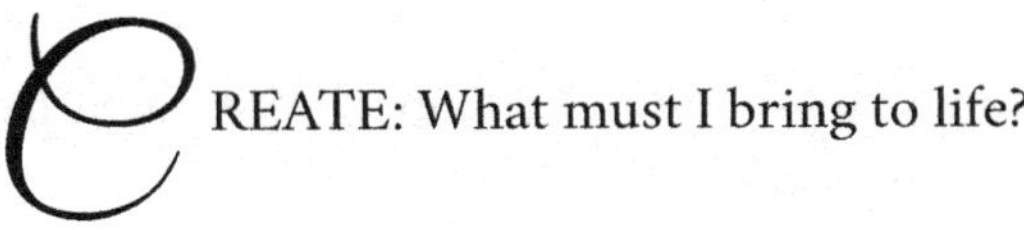REATE: What must I bring to life?

IMPROVE: What requires improvement to enhance its success?

REMOVE: What obstacles need to be dealt with, stored away or removed completely from my life?

ACCEPT: What is out of my control and needs to be influenced or accepted?

PUTTING RHYME 9 INTO ACTION

In what events today was I the Developer, and was the approach I took successful:

1. Event:
2. Approach:
3. Success:

RHYME X
SPEND WISELY

RHYME 10

SPEND WISELY

The borrower is always slave to the lender,

---

freedom doesn't come from being a spender.

SPEND WISELY

We spend money to solve two problems: a need or a desire.

A need is necessary for living,

---

whereas, meeting a desire may temporarily excite us or impress others.

PREPARATION FOR USING RHYME 10

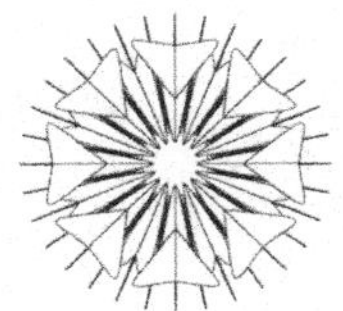

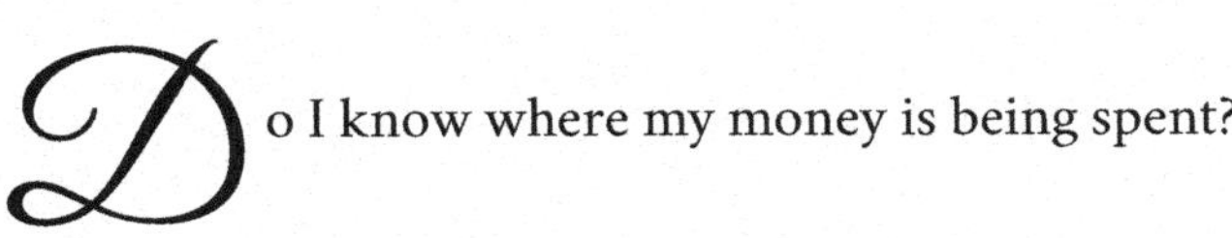

Do I know where my money is being spent?

LIST MY EXPENSES next to the following two categories:

Necessities:

Desires:

WHAT SPECIFICALLY IS my area for spending?

WHAT FEELINGS AM I trying to attain by satisfying these desires?

HOW ELSE COULD I achieve this same feeling without the cost?

PUTTING RHYME 10 INTO ACTION

Tips to limit spending:

- Each pay, set a budget of physical cash for 'desire' spending and when it runs out, no more spending.
- Earmark any planned excess cash and transfer it into a minimum withdrawal savings account, shares, or other money-holding, interest-related account on the day you receive pay.

In what ways have I deliberately limited my opportunities to spend 'desire' money?

EVERY INVESTMENT or withdrawal is incremental and compounds, whether positively when saved or negatively in debt. Decide now, the strategies I will use to reduce my spending and begin saving.

RHYME XI
BE RESOURCEFUL

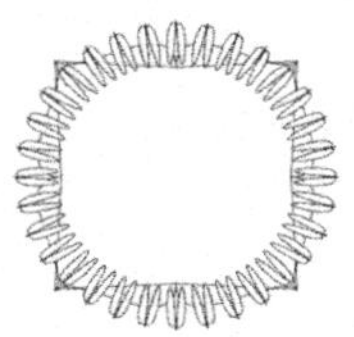

RHYME 11

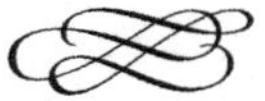

BE RESOURCEFUL

As nothing will ever be enough,

---

don't seek comfort in physical stuff.

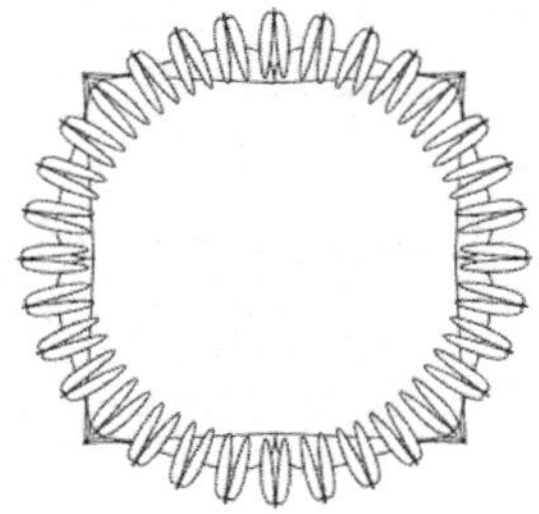

BE RESOURCEFUL

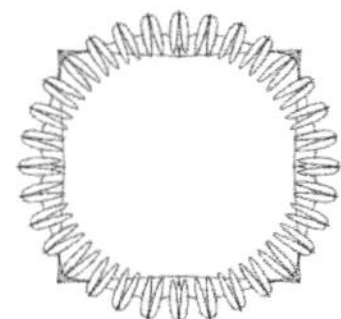

The "happiness highs" from purchasing new stuff can evaporate quickly, often leaving a feeling of "buyer's remorse".

Contentment comes from the challenge of being resourceful

---

with the items you already possess.

PREPARATION FOR USING RHYME 11

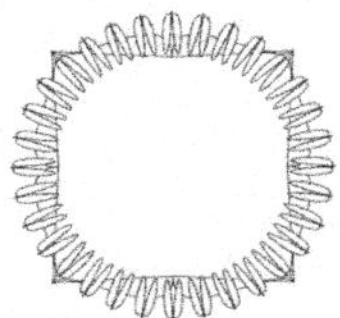

Every commitment comes at a cost, i.e. a financial loss, extra responsibility, emotional response, or a digital, mental or physical cluttering of my precious time and space.

HOW MANY ITEMS do I estimate I own and is it excessive?

CONSIDER the following questions for your possessions:

- Why do I have this in my life?
- Does it bring great pleasure to possess it or use it?
- Does it serve an important purpose?
- Is it just a past fashion, hobby or fantasy-self that I no longer pursue and it now clutters space?
- I don't need it now but could I replace it if I needed it again?

PUTTING RHYME 11 INTO ACTION

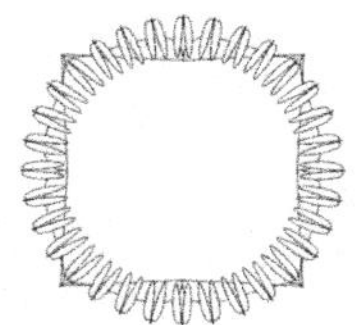

What did I feel tempted to spend money on today?

WHAT MARKETED, promised feeling does it give to 'improve my life' and entice me to spend money on it? Do I believe it?

WHAT IS the cost to me, or others, of possessing this?

DO I still really need this? How will I justify this?

RHYME XII
SEEK QUIET

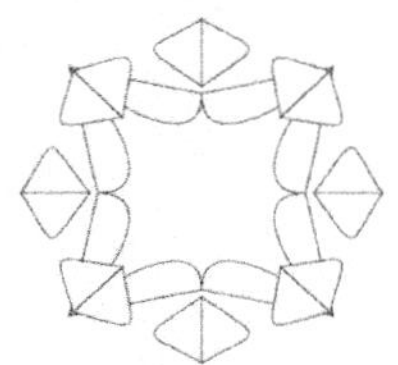

RHYME 12

SEEK QUIET

When you feel the overload,

---

a quiet space is the antidote.

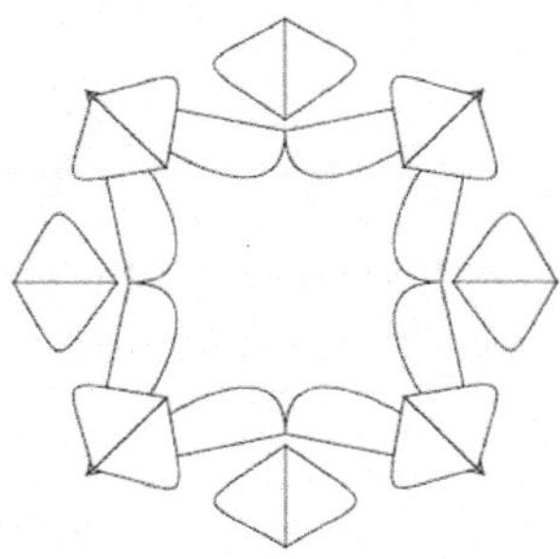

SEEK QUIET

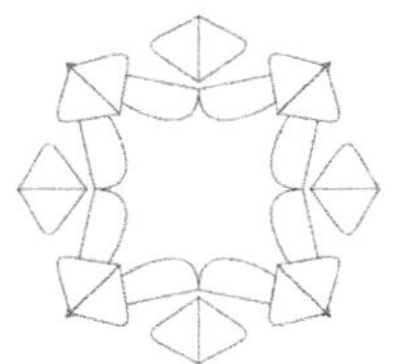

Quiet allows us to lose the distractions, noise and busyness of our thoughts that often lead to overwhelm,

---

frustration and confusion.

Quiet reveals the repetitive messages of our past and future concerns, that absorb us daily, as they wait for resolution.

PREPARATION FOR USING RHYME 12

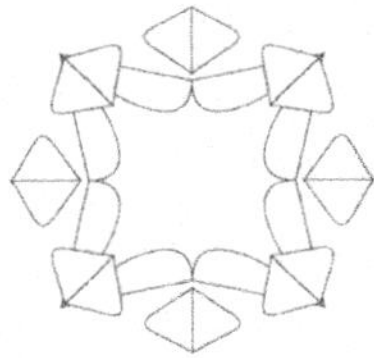

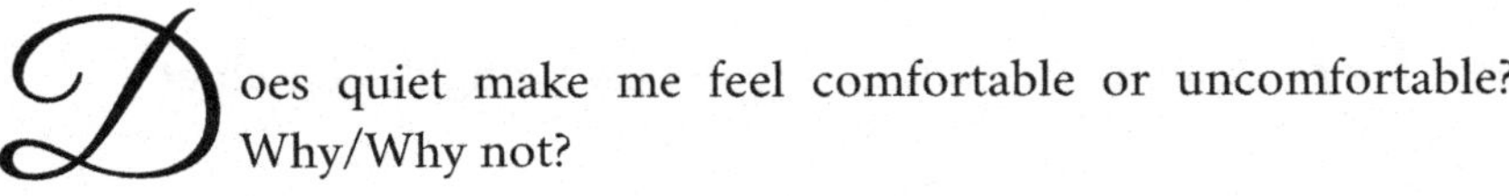

Does quiet make me feel comfortable or uncomfortable? Why/Why not?

When I am in a quiet moment, where do I notice the stress and tension in my body has gathered, as a result of my busy life?

When and where are my quiet moments and can I plan to retreat to them as I need to?

PUTTING RHYME 12 INTO ACTION

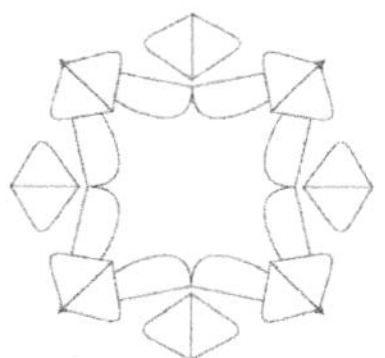

In a quiet moment, where did my thoughts go today?

HOW DID I feel about being in quiet?

ARE my feelings telling me something that needs changing, improving or accepting, regarding myself or my lifestyle?

HOW COULD I IMPROVE A 'QUIET MOMENT' experience for next time?

RHYME XIII
HAVE FEWER WORRIES

RHYME 13

HAVE FEW WORRIES

Disregard all your negative thoughts,

---

for outside of your head they stand for nought.

HAVE FEWER WORRIES

Thoughts are fantasies of the future or assumptions from the past.

They pick at us bit-by-bit, as if to make themselves valid.

Only accept this moment as real.

PREPARATION FOR USING RHYME 13

What frequent negative thoughts that I tend to have.

Do they come from past worries or worries about the future?

---

1. Negative Thought:
2. Is it a Past Worry, Future Worry or both?:
3. What do I need to do to bring my thought to the present moment where I have control?

PUTTING RHYME 13 INTO ACTION

Today I can disempower negative thoughts by imagining:

1. Labelling my thoughts as 'past' or 'future' and letting them drift by without judgement.
2. Scrunching a negative image into a tiny speck and tossing it in the bin; showering it with colourful petals; over-exposing it with bright light; cutting it up with scissors; or smashing it into a million pieces.
3. Hearing a negative comment in a higher pitch until it sounds funny.
4. Reversing the direction of an unpleasant feeling churning inside; lightening a heavy feeling or tickling it; or completely squeezing it out of my body.

What did I do to reduce the impact of negative thoughts today?

RHYME XIV
CHOOSE TRUTH

RHYME 14

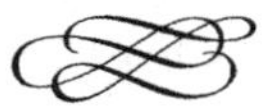

CHOOSE TRUTH

Which is worthy of giving your time to,

your fantasy self or your self that's true?

CHOOSE TRUTH

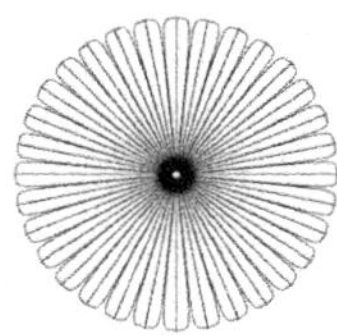

We all live fantasy lives in our daydreams. Our real truth is what we positively pursue in our day-to-day lives as reality; not what we escape from.

English Romantic Poet John Keats wrote in "Ode on a Grecian Urn"

"Beauty is truth, truth beauty, - that is all
Ye know on earth, and all ye need to know."

PREPARATION FOR USING RHYME 14

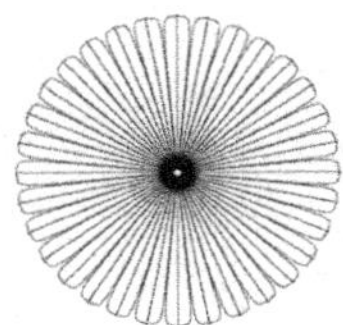

What are my fantasy selves related to the hobbies, lifestyles or careers I dream about?

Do these fantasy selves detrimentally rob my joy, time, money, thoughts or space that would be better invested somewhere more realistic and worthwhile?

What do these fantasy selves represent to me in terms of feelings or desires I want to experience?

What more realistic and practical ways can I get these same feelings?

PUTTING RHYME 14 INTO ACTION

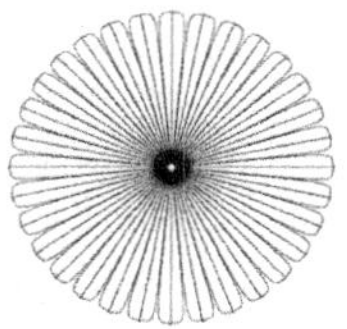

Every time a fantasy self comes up ask:

- Should I sacrifice the time, money and space needed to indulge in this fantasy?
- What am I avoiding or escaping by indulging in this fantasy?
- On what realistic interest could my time or money be better spent?

WHAT WERE the different fantasies that came into my thoughts today?

RHYME XV
THINGS TAKE TIME

RHYME 15

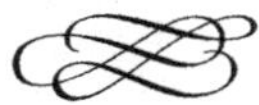

THINGS TAKE TIME

In a world that moves fast and has instant demands,

---

knowing Things Take Time is the patient stance.

THINGS TAKE TIME

Where quantity is a reaction to meet the deadlines of instant gratification for solutions,

---

RIGHT NOW,

---

quality achieves refinement through time, artistry and thought.

PREPARATION FOR USING RHYME 15

In what instances in my life do I expect instant gratification?

AM I reasonable in my expectations for instant solutions?

DO I expect others to cater to my demands?

WHERE WOULD I like to exercise more patience and deliver a quality performance over 'just good enough'?

WHAT MASS-MARKET and low-quality things do I possess that I could replace with a single, less-consumable, higher quality item?

PUTTING RHYME 15 INTO ACTION

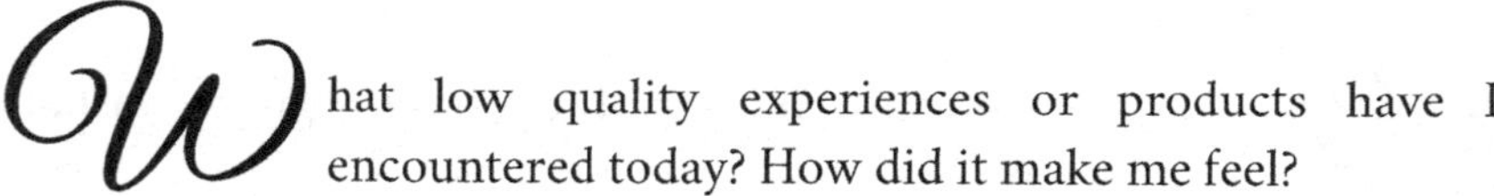

What low quality experiences or products have I encountered today? How did it make me feel?

When did I put in a quality performance today? How did it make me feel?

Did it take longer than I expected?

How reasonable were my expectations of products, services or another's performance today?

What do I need to do or think to improve my expectations?

RHYME XVI
CLEAR BOUNDARIES

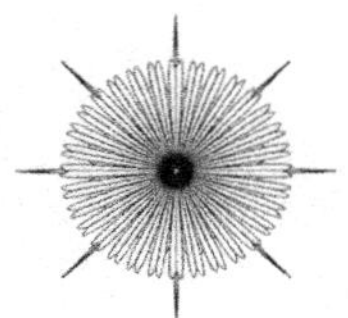

RHYME 16

CLEAR BOUNDARIES

Mark your boundaries with clear expectations,

---

stand-up to trespassers without hesitation.

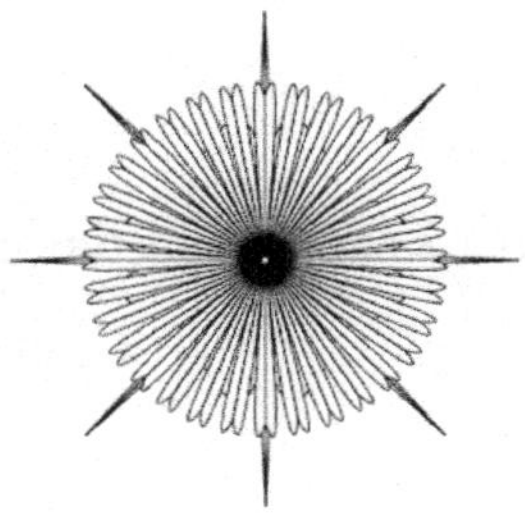

CLEAR BOUNDARIES

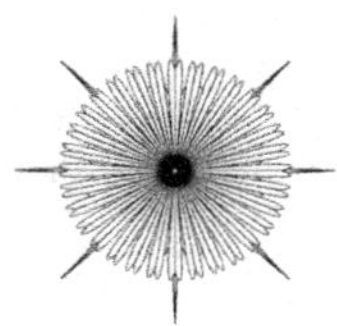

People will always test your boundaries, and some will look for a weakness to exploit.

Don't be the victim of others' unreasonable expectations of you,

---

nor have unreasonable expectations of others.

PREPARATION FOR USING RHYME 16

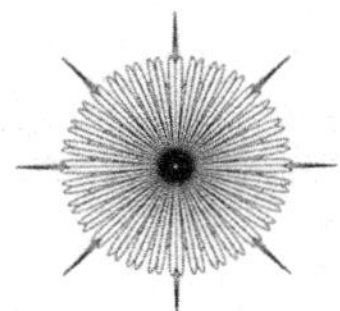

What are my boundaries which I will defend if they are crossed:

- Boundaries for my beliefs?
- Boundaries for my family?
- Boundaries for my self-esteem and worth?
- Boundaries for my personal space?
- Boundaries for my ____________________ ?

WHERE HAVE my boundaries originated (are they mine or someone else's?) and are they reasonable and realistic?

PUTTING RHYME 16 INTO ACTION

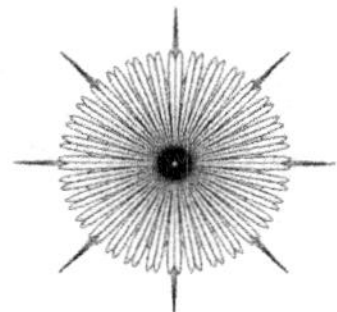

I only have control over my own attitudes and actions. I am say "No" to unreasonable expectations.

What did I say a willing 'Yes' to today, and why?

What did I say "No" to today? Why did I say "No"?

Did I say "maybe" or "Possibly" as an answer? Why?

Are there any issues around my assertiveness that I need to address? What are they?

RHYME XVII
SEIZE MOMENTS

RHYME 17

SEIZE THE MOMENT

Is this the best use of my current time?

How can I make this moment mine?

SEIZE MOMENTS

Give priority to what's important and don't allow minor 'busy-work' to consume your valuable time.

Stoic Roman Emperor, Marcus Aurelius (121-180 AD) said,

"You're better off not giving the small things more time than they deserve."

PREPARATION FOR USING RHYME 17

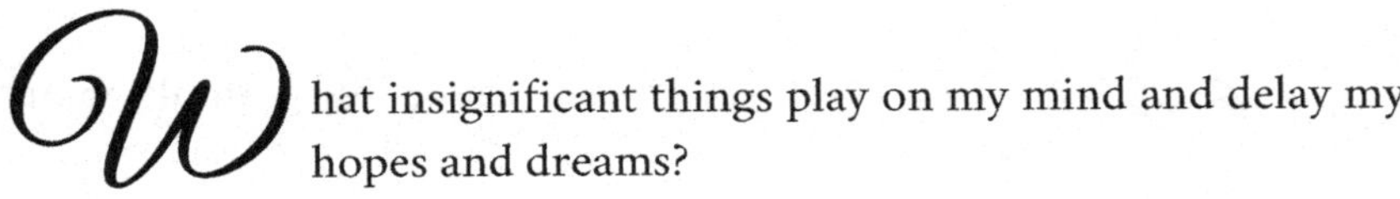

What insignificant things play on my mind and delay my hopes and dreams?

What do I value as important in this moment of my life?

What 'busy-work' do I turn to as an excuse not to work on the important things in life?

What am I avoiding through 'busy-work' and Why?

PUTTING RHYME 17 INTO ACTION

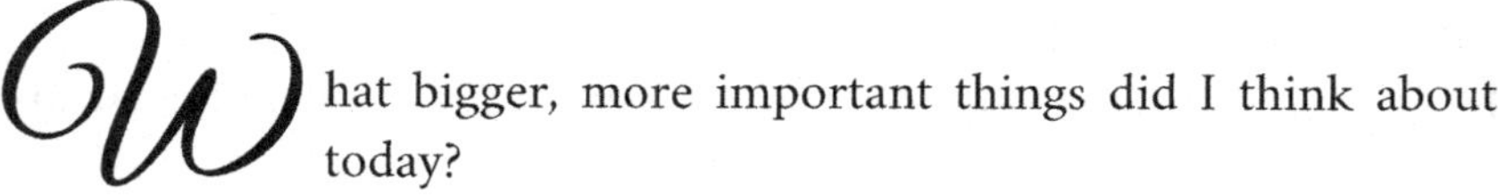

What bigger, more important things did I think about today?

WHAT 'BUSYWORK' did I create for myself or accepted from others?

WHAT IMPORTANT TASKS did I focus on today and did I feel satisfied by what I accomplished?

HOW CAN I improve the time spent on the important things or the quality of my practice?

RHYME XVIII
UNDIVIDED ATTENTION

RHYME 18

UNDIVIDED ATTENTION

When meeting others don't over-share,

---

make simple small talk, listen and care.

UNDIVIDED ATTENTION

If you care for those around you,

---

give your undivided attention;

---

good friends will do the same for you.

PREPARATION FOR USING RHYME 18

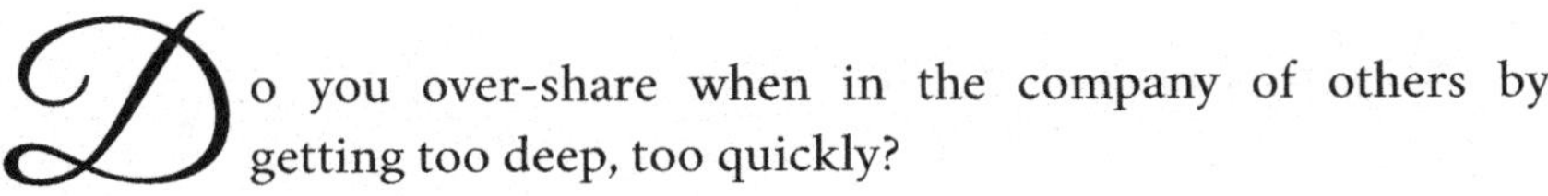

Do you over-share when in the company of others by getting too deep, too quickly?

WHAT PERCENTAGE of a conversation do you think you dominate and what talk do you tend to dominate the conversation with?

IN WHAT WAYS might you come across as too open?

IN WHAT WAYS might you come across as too closed or cold?

PUTTING RHYME 18 INTO ACTION

In a conversation I had today:

- I spoke for ______% of the time.
- Did I Actively Listen?
- Did I Smile and nod?
- Did I use small talk about shared surroundings or small relatable events?

WHAT POSITIVE STEPS did I take when conversing with others today?

WHAT CONVERSATIONAL SKILLS could I improve for tomorrow?

RHYME XIX
CHOOSE GOOD

RHYME 19

CHOOSE GOOD

Good things...in!

---

bad things...bin!

CHOOSE GOOD

Good is a higher standard for which to aspire.

Be guided by your moral compass for your peace of mind,

---

and the peace of mind of others.

PREPARATION FOR USING RHYME 19

What negative feelings that I need to address are related to:

1. WINNING OTHERS' approval?

2. Expecting to be treated fairly and kindly?

3. Having things my way?

WHAT BENEFIT DO I get from allowing these negative responses to occur?

PUTTING RHYME 19 INTO ACTION

Negative thoughts about a criticism are just my interpretation of the event. I need to strengthen my resilience, be assertive and not allow bad interpretations to disempower me.

To build my response to criticism I will ask:

- I'm interested in the source of your information?
- What makes your evidence true, or the person it has come from an authority?
- Where is it written in the rules that it has to be this way?
- Am I not allowed the right to have a different opinion?

To prepare for responding to future events, I will modify strong feelings, such as 'I'm angry' to "I'm a little annoyed but I can handle it and turn things around!"

WHAT OTHER STRONG negative feelings can I modify?

RHYME XX
BEST EFFORT

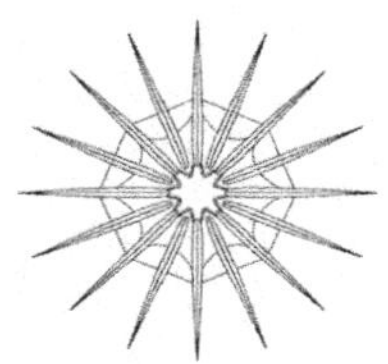

RHYME 20

BEST EFFORT

You'll never be perfect and that's ok,

---

just give it your best day-to-day.

BEST EFFORT

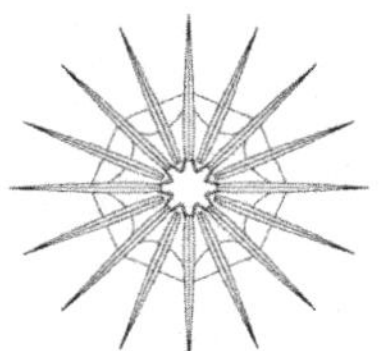

Giving your best effort in the moment is all you can do.

Be proud of yourself for making the effort regardless of the results.

Results are only feedback and another chance to improve your performance.

PREPARATION FOR USING RHYME 20

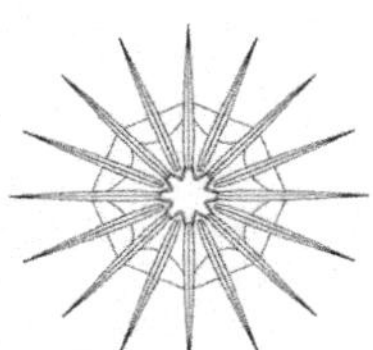

Life is a process, and is not exact. I can still aim for quality without having to be perfect; it is human to err.

IN WHAT AREAS of my life do I expect to be perfect for myself and for others?

MYSELF:

OTHERS:

WHY DO I care so much about getting things exactly right?

PUTTING RHYME 20 INTO ACTION

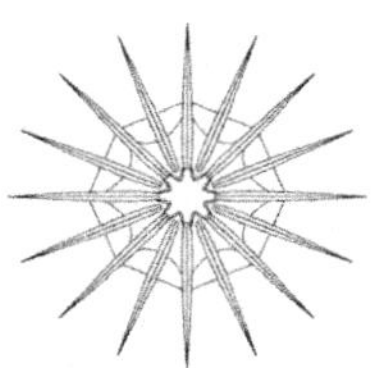

What have I put my best effort into today?

Have I felt disappointed over anything I have tackled today?

Why have I felt this way?

Have I felt satisfied with my effort in a task today?

How exactly did it make me feel?

RHYME XXI
EMOTIONS PASS

RHYME 21

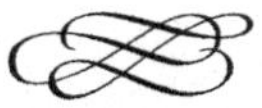

EMOTIONS PASS

Emotions are simply energy in motion,

ebbing and flowing like waves on the ocean.

EMOTIONS PASS

Accept that emotions will influence your thoughts, feelings, behaviours, moods and motivations.

Learn to regulate them for healthy interactions but not suppress them to the detriment of your well-being.

Know that they will pass with time.

PREPARATION FOR USING RHYME 21

Negative emotions occur as a reaction to an actual or perceived loss; such as, losing the approval of someone, losing an expected privilege, losing a sense of justice by feeling a rule has been broken, simply not getting things your way, or losing someone familiar from your life.

WHAT EMOTIONS DO I experience which I consider to be negative? Why are they negative experiences?

WHAT FEELINGS DO I experience after displaying negative emotions in front of others?

PUTTING RHYME 21 INTO ACTION

If an emotional outburst is brewing, I will calm down by:

- biting my tongue
- taking a deep breath in, holding it, breathing slowly out
- pinching a thumb and a finger together
- repeating to myself, "Calm and composed"

What negative emotions did I experience today?

How did I reduce the intensity of these emotions?

How can I handle my negative emotions better tomorrow?

RHYME XXII
GET MOVING

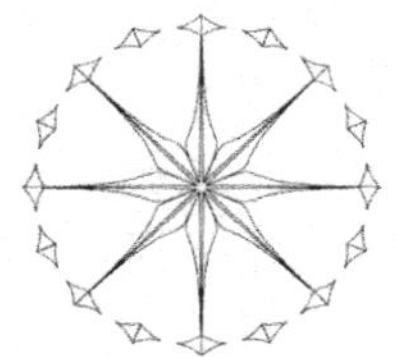

RHYME 22

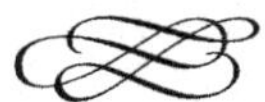

GET MOVING

When you're stuck in a rut and you need some traction,

---

break down that task, take 5 minutes of action.

GET MOVING

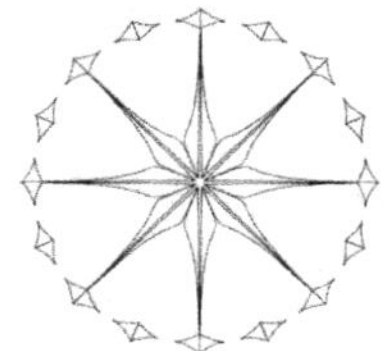

When it's difficult to start a task, divide it into all its separate actions.

Start the very first action for five minutes only.

You may find five minutes becomes more!

PREPARATION FOR USING RHYME 22

What projects do I have that I have not moved forward yet?

CHOOSE one of my projects and break it down into all its separate actions.

PUTTING RHYME 22 INTO ACTION

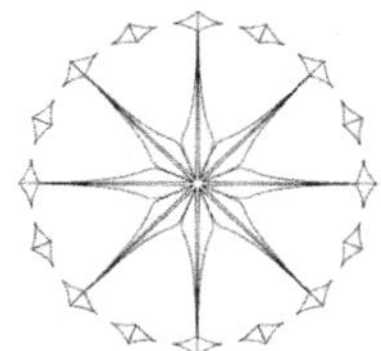

I will set a timer for five minutes every time I catch myself saying statements such as, "Later", "Not now", "I can't be bothered". I will be disciplined, and get up and complete those five minutes. I know that no-one really likes to start, but it makes all the difference to those who make it a practice.

Did my 5 minutes turn into further minutes?

Did any challenging thoughts stop me getting started?

What distractions must I now completely remove?

RHYME XXIII
TAKE COURAGE

RHYME 23

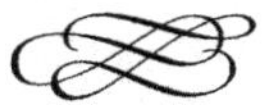

TAKE COURAGE

Courage comes in the face of adversity,

---

draw on your principles and unwavering certainty.

TAKE COURAGE

To be able to do something in the face of fear and danger,

---

requires your inner strength, capabilities,

---

beliefs, and values.

PREPARATION FOR USING RHYME 23

hat do I fear?

WHAT ARE these fears protecting me from physically and emotionally?

IN WHAT AREAS of my life would I like to show courage?

WHAT WOULD I have to risk to show this courage?

PUTTING RHYME 23 INTO ACTION

When feelings of fear or anxiety arise today, ask:
"What is the worst that can happen?"

When have I had to be even the slightest bit resilient and brave today?

What have my fears been centred around today, either real or imagined?

Physical harm, losing approval, humiliation, emotional hurt, failure, success etc.

When could I have been more courageous today?

RHYME XXIV
BRAVERY THROUGH COMPASSION

RHYME 24

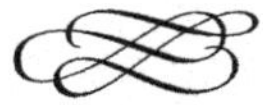

BRAVERY THROUGH COMPASSION

Bravery is a self-less action,

---

helping others through sincere compassion.

BRAVERY THROUGH COMPASSION

Bravery is the ability to confront danger and threat despite fear.

When compassion for others is foremost in mind,

---

fear is furthest from concern.

PREPARATION FOR USING RHYME 24

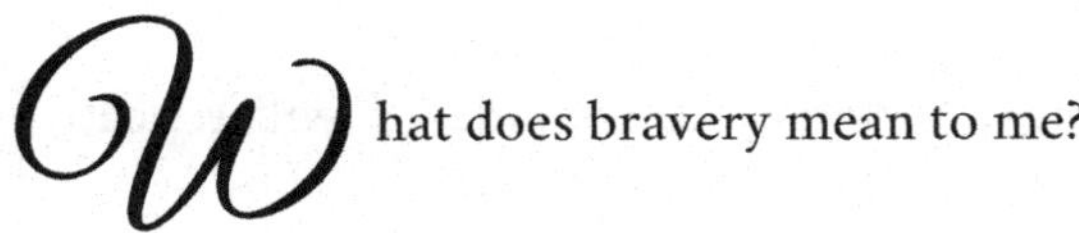

What does bravery mean to me?

WHO DO I consider to be brave and in what way exactly are they brave?

WHAT REASSURANCES AM I able to offer others who need compassion?

WHO CAN I reach out to now with compassion?

PUTTING RHYME 24 INTO ACTION

If something uncomfortable occurs today, I will repeat "I can do this!", and act.

In what uncomfortable situations was I brave today?

What uncomfortable situations did I avoid and why was I afraid?

Who was I able to offer compassion to and what was their reaction?

How did this make me feel?

RHYME XXV
FORGIVE MISTAKES

RHYME 25

FORGIVE MISTAKES

Kindly reflect on your past,

---

never judge nor be too harsh.

FORGIVE MISTAKES

We must learn from past mistakes, rather than punishing ourselves with guilt, embarrassment, fear or regret; within the layers of our memories we all find mistakes.

The past is history, the future a mystery.

Concentrate on your present behaviours as they are all you can change.

PREPARATION FOR USING RHYME 25

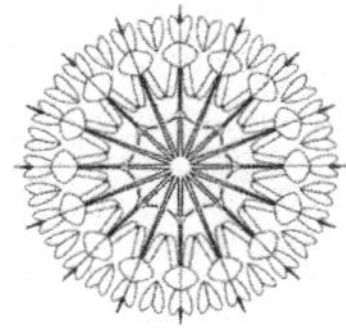

o I hold onto guilt or regret about issues from my past?

ARE they at a level where I need to seek professional guidance from a counsellor or psychologist? Or can I take control of them myself?

WHAT POSITIVE, learning perspective do I need to take from these past mistakes and realistically apply to my life right now?

PUTTING RHYME 25 INTO ACTION

If a past thought intrudes in a negative way, I will say to myself,
"Yesterday is history, what counts is right now."
What other positive phrases could I say?

DID any negative past events come to my mind this week?

WHAT FEELINGS DID THEY TRIGGER?

WHAT ARE these memories trying to tell me and what constructive lesson can I learn from them now?

RHYME XXVI
KEEP PERSISTING

RHYME 26

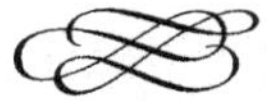

KEEP PERSISTING

When a large obstacle stands in your way,

---

keep chipping at it day-by-day.

KEEP PERSISTING

If you truly want to follow through on a course of action or an opinion,

---

keep chipping away,

---

despite the obstacles you find along your path.

PREPARATION FOR USING RHYME 26

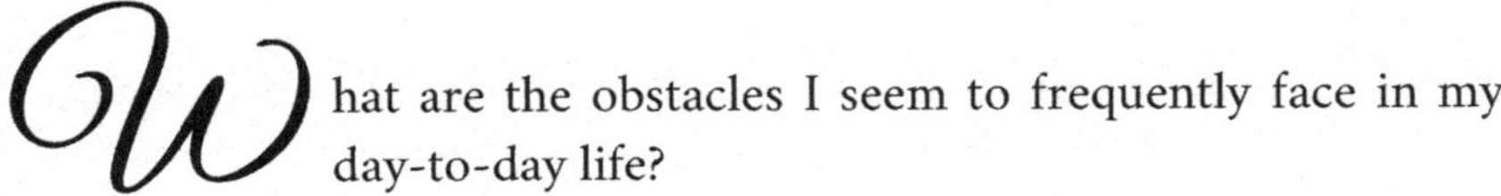

What are the obstacles I seem to frequently face in my day-to-day life?

What different approaches do I use to get around them?

What other possible approaches could I take?

What obstacles do I have a low tolerance for that makes me give up?

What do I need to do to build my resilience to handle this low tolerance?

PUTTING RHYME 26 INTO ACTION

This week, if you find yourself giving up early or too easily, say one of the following phrases to yourself:

- "Keep moving forward!"
- "Keep on Keeping on!"
- "Just one more!"

WHAT ALTERNATE APPROACH did I take today when I felt my path was blocked by an obstacle?

RHYME XXVII
GREATER PURPOSE

RHYME 27

GREATER PURPOSE

You can never please all your audience,

---

your greater purpose is more glorious.

GREATER PURPOSE

You will gain approval from everyone for the greater purpose of the life you lead, you may even offend some.

There are many tribes in this world, all with differing views.

There is also at least one group out there for whom you belong, reach out and find it!

PREPARATION FOR USING RHYME 27

What is my greater purpose, no matter how simple or complicated it might be?

Why do I think this purpose is important?

I am willing to pursue my beliefs, opinions and practices with like-minded people; however, I should expect my view will conflict with at least somebody, at some point.

- What personal pursuits and beliefs do I have that I know could cause disagreement with others?
- How do I approach those whose opinions differ?

Which like-minded group can I reach out to?

PUTTING RHYME 27 INTO ACTION

I am prepared to treat others views with respect today, knowing that they may not respect mine. If they wish to discuss it, I will listen but affirm my beliefs and whether they are persuaded or not, that is okay.

WHAT SITUATIONS CAME up today when I needed to listen to the viewpoint of another or express mine?

WHAT WAS the outcome of the situation?

DID I have any reflections today on my greater purpose in life? What comes to mind now? If I were to cease living, what realistic action would I regret not having acted on?

RHYME XXVIII
CALMING BREATH

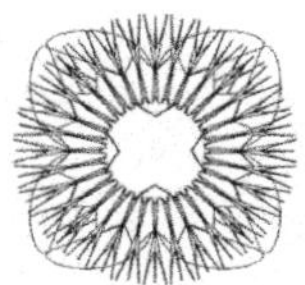

RHYME 28

CALMING BREATH

One deep breath in, and out on 10,

---

will help you start in balance again.

CALMING BREATH

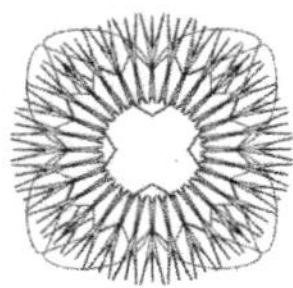

If your emotions get the best of you in times of confusion, worry, distraction or overwhelm,

---

breathe in for ten seconds, hold for five

---

and out for ten.

PREPARATION FOR USING RHYME 28

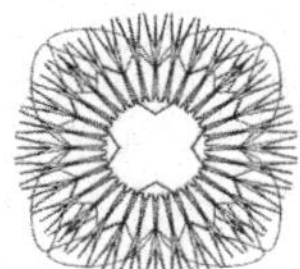

In what situations do I find myself flustered, frustrated, stressed or anxious?

WHAT TRIGGERS THESE FEELINGS?

WHAT OPPORTUNITIES EXIST where I can take a few deep breaths to relax and centre myself in the moment, away from intrusive past and future thoughts? e.g. on a break, while travelling, in a waiting room, on waking, just before sleep etc.

PUTTING RHYME 28 INTO ACTION

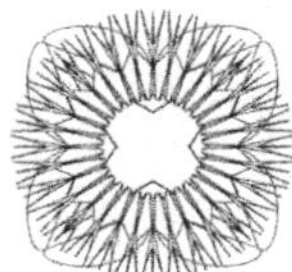

I will make it a goal to take some deep breaths at least twice today.

AT WHAT TIMES today and in what situations did I find it easier to take some deep breaths?

DID the breaths help me in any noticeable way?

DO I need a reminder or trigger to take some breaths. What will I use?

e.g. electronic/digital, a schedule, a chair or sofa I sit on, or a space I enter etc.

RHYME XXIX
EVER-CHANGING JOURNEY

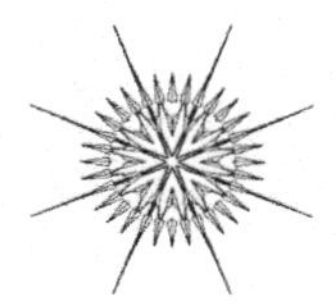

RHYME 29

EVER-CHANGING JOURNEY

If you can't find a straight line from A to B,

---

then journey from A B C D to E.

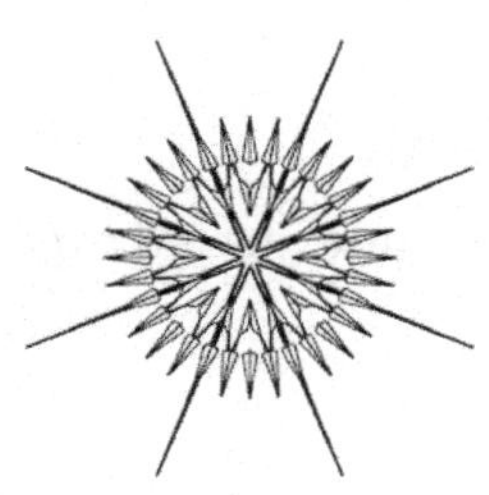

EVER-CHANGING JOURNEY

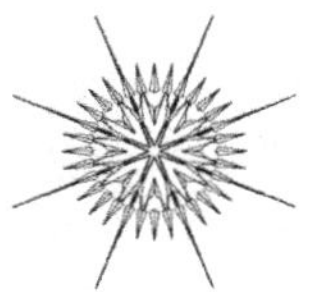

Very few journeys we take in life are linear, from point 'a' to point 'b'.
We are often required to take detours.

Though our journey may be longer,

---

our learning through unexpected experience is stronger.

PREPARATION FOR USING RHYME 29

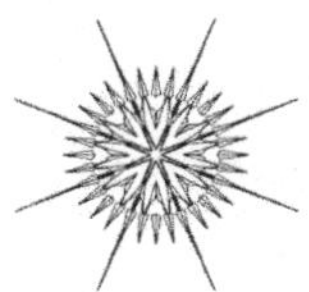

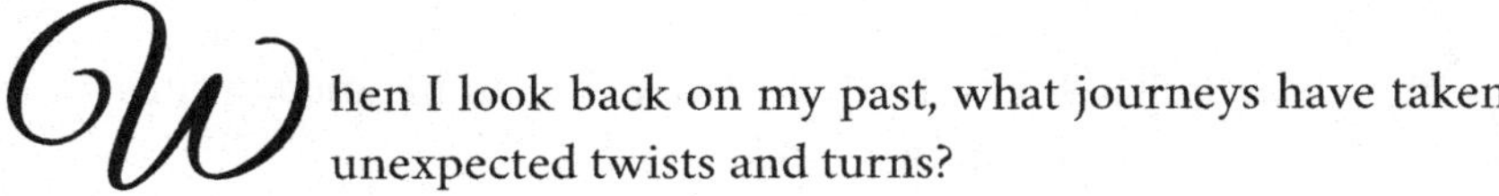

hen I look back on my past, what journeys have taken unexpected twists and turns?

What journey am I on right now that has already taken a different route than expected?

Do I expect to be taking any different paths soon?

PUTTING RHYME 29 INTO ACTION

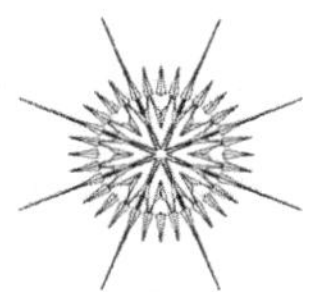

Expect that I will possibly be taking unplanned routes in a venture I take on this week.

SAY THE FOLLOWING TO MYSELF, "This is not what I planned but it is to be expected. These things happen."

WHAT CHANGES HAVE I made to a task today?

HOW DID I feel about taking a different route?

WHAT PERSONAL RESOURCES do I need to draw on to handle unexpected changes?

RHYME XXX
DO OR DO NOT

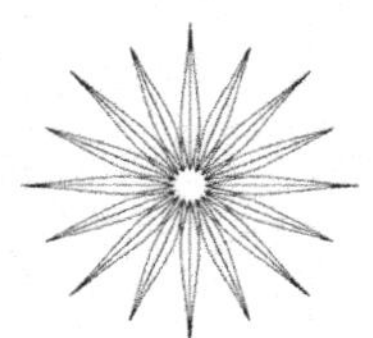

RHYME 30

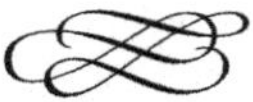

DO OR DO NOT

Do or do not,

———

the only choice that you have got.

DO OR DO NOT

You can either get on and do something or decide not to.

By deciding not to, you are ironically doing something.

Undone situations will grow and multiply and so too will your stress, guilt and anxiety.

PREPARATION FOR USING RHYME 30

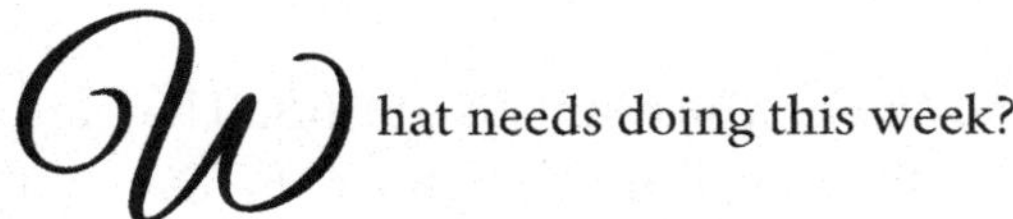

What needs doing this week?

What do I predict may stop me from completing or not even starting each action?

How can I prepare for interruptions to my actions?

PUTTING RHYME 30 INTO ACTION

Always tackle first, the things you want to put off. They are likely the tasks that will haunt you throughout the day and have a cost in terms of time, money and undesirable feelings. If they are left undone, the consequences and angst, will multiply.

Invite myself to the challenge, roll up my sleeves and say, "Let's do this!"

WHAT ACTIONS HAVE I completed from my preparation list?

WHAT DID I NOT COMPLETE? Why?

WHAT UNEXPECTED THINGS popped up that I had to take action on? Were they important or distractions?

RHYME XXXI
SELF-RELIANCE

RHYME 31

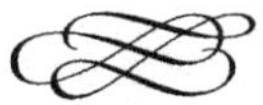

SELF-RELIANCE

If you were your only caring best friend,

---

what advice would you give yourself to change or mend?

SELF-RELIANCE

We often look after family and friends better than we look after ourselves.

Be a friend to yourself

---

and be brave enough to reach out when you need support.

PREPARATION FOR USING RHYME 31

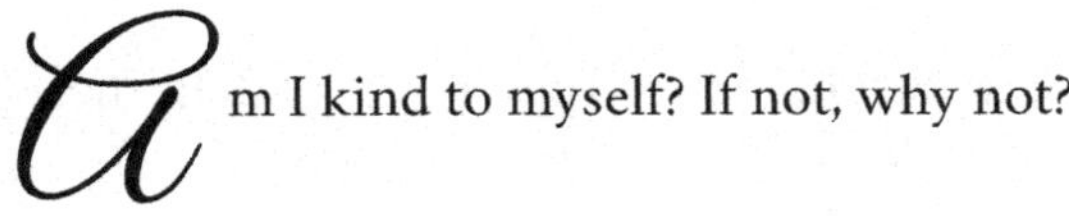

Am I kind to myself? If not, why not?

WHAT DO I say to myself that is kind?

WHAT NEGATIVE THINGS do I say about myself?

WHAT IS the reason behind the negative comments?

HOW CAN I re-word these comments into encouraging statements?

PUTTING RHYME 31 INTO ACTION

Today, if I say any of the following, I will catch these thoughts and turn them around.

- "I'm not good enough" or "I can't do it" to "I will do my very best" or "I can give it a go"
- "I don't know what I'm doing" to "I will learn from practising or studying"
- "I'm stupid" to "I have faith that I can get this"
- "I can't cope" to "I am stronger than I think"
- "I'm a horrible person" to "I have been kind many times in the past"

WHAT NEGATIVE COMMENTS have I thought about myself today?

HOW HAVE I turned those negatives into positives, and if not, what could I say to myself now?

RHYME XXXII
SMALL INVESTMENTS

RHYME 32

SMALL INVESTMENTS

As time continues slipping away,

---

try improving one thing every day.

SMALL INVESTMENTS

One little daily investment in the form of an action is how we progress in each area of life.

As all these actions compound,

---

our investment grows.

PREPARATION FOR USING RHYME 32

After World War 2, Japan rebuilt their devastated economy through the principal of 'Kaizen'. Our nearest interpretation is "change for the better" or "constant improvement".

WHAT LITTLE ACTIONS do I need to schedule in every day to ensure my own constant improvement in the following life areas?

- Health and Fitness:
- Relationships:
- Finances:
- Career:
- Education:
- Spirituality or Personal Development:

PUTTING RHYME 32 INTO ACTION

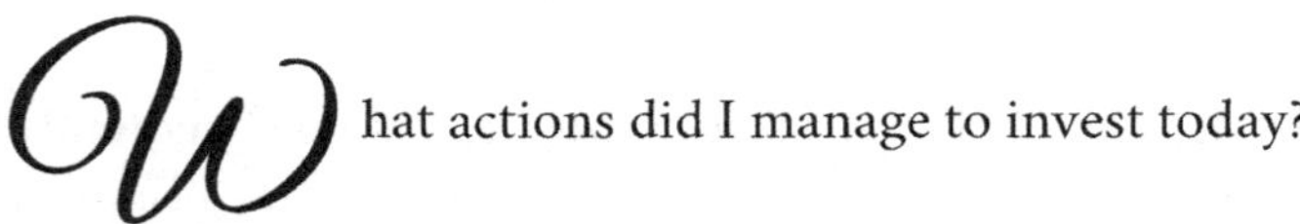

What actions did I manage to invest today?

Which actions did I miss and how will I make them up before tomorrow?

Are there any other actions I would like to add to my routine?

RHYME XXXIII
CHOOSE FREEDOM

RHYME 33

CHOOSE FREEDOM

If all you want is another's agreement,

---

you'll see criticism as bad and you'll make no improvement.

CHOOSE FREEDOM

Seeking approval will lead you into dependence on others. Your esteem, confidence and worth mustn't be tied to others' opinions of you.

To be independent from seeking outside approval,

---

is to be truly free.

PREPARATION FOR USING RHYME 33

How do I typically react when someone criticises or questions me?

WHAT IS the reason behind my reaction?

WHAT SEQUENCE of feelings do I go through after criticism?

ARE THERE MORE constructive ways I can use criticisms to improve myself? How?

PUTTING RHYME 33 INTO ACTION

If I feel that I am being criticised this week, I will:

- Stop and not react with my first response.
- Listen for the benefit of feedback.
- Feed back a summary of what they have said, "I hear that you are saying that you want me to..."
- Ask for specific examples behind the criticism.
- Acknowledge anything you actually have done.
- State that this is an isolated incident and ask for ideas for handling things differently in future.
- Ask for time to reflect on the issues for next steps and schedule a follow-up discussion.
- If random criticism comes from a stranger or an abusive person, apologise anyway, unfair or not, and shrug it off. It's their problem and they might react unpredictably with aggression if challenged.

How did I handle criticism today?

RHYME XXXIV
YOU FIT

RHYME 34

YOU FIT

There is a lid for every pot,

---

some fit snugly, some do not.

YOU FIT

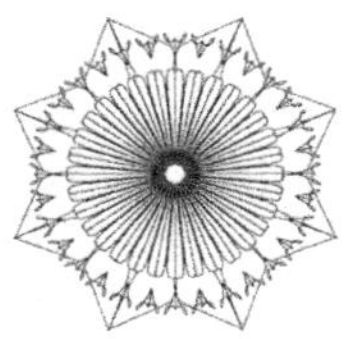

There are people, jobs and places for us all. Some situations just don't fit us, nor we fit them. The discomfort we feel is a warning signal that something is just not the right fit.

You cannot force ill-fitting circumstances upon yourself,

---

nor anyone else.

PREPARATION FOR USING RHYME 34

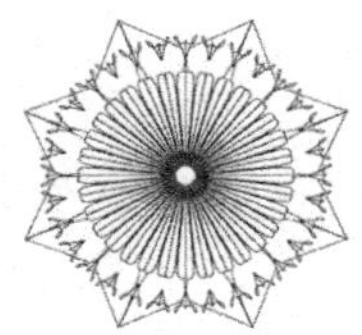

After trying it for a reasonable time, does this situation, relationship, job, environment, belief, fit right with me?

WHAT DO I think would better suit me?

Is this a realistic and achievable desire or just a fantasy?

PUTTING RHYME 34 INTO ACTION

I will not burn all my bridges until I have explored my options and made my exit plan.

WHAT CAN I do right now to explore something that fits me more suitably?

HOW HAVE others achieved what I desire?

WHAT APPROACHES CAN I model from these people?

RHYME XXXV
YOU'RE RESPONSIBLE

RHYME 35

YOU'RE RESPONSIBLE

Seldom complain, rarely explain,

from all excuses you must refrain.

YOU'RE RESPONSIBLE

To be responsible is to handle issues in a constructive way. Own any mistakes you make.

To avoid disappointment and blame, lower your expectations of others;

---

instead, influence them by being a role-model for higher standards.

PREPARATION FOR USING RHYME 35

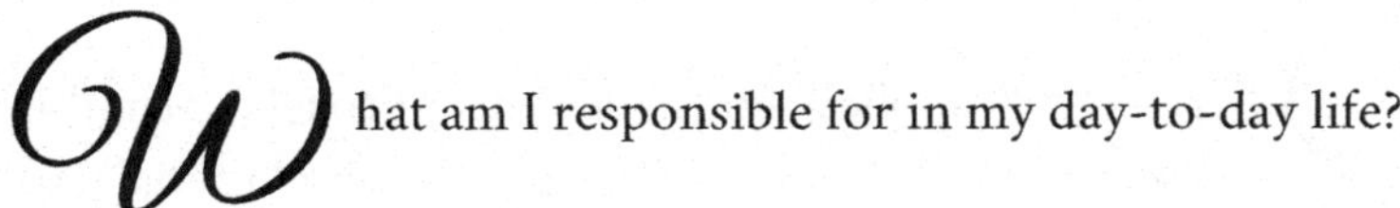

What am I responsible for in my day-to-day life?

WHAT EXPECTATIONS DO I project onto others whom I have no actual control over?

PUTTING RHYME 35 INTO ACTION

What have I applied constructive approaches to this week rather than criticising, complaining or condemning?

Have I felt disappointment in another person this week?

What were my expectations of them?

What gives me the right to have these expectations of them? Are they too high?

How can I explain this to them in a civil way?

RHYME XXXVI
TAKE RISKS

RHYME 36

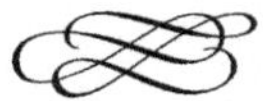

TAKE RISKS

Comfort entices you to sit on your butt,

---

discomfort shifts you out of your rut.

TAKE RISKS

Change involves risks:

---

new people, new places, new behaviours, new learning, and new circumstances.

We often sacrifice long-term growth for short-term comfort and instant gratification.

PREPARATION FOR USING RHYME 36

hat comfort traps entice me to sit about rather than getting up and moving?

WHAT DO I find uncomfortable on a scale out of 10, 10 being the most uncomfortable and 0 being completely comfortable?

- 10/10:
- 9/10:
- 8/10:
- 7/10:
- 6/10:
- 5/10:
- 4/10:
- 3/10:
- 2/10:
- 1/10:
- 0:

PUTTING RHYME 36 INTO ACTION

If I am feeling trapped by comfort but guilty for a task I need to get done, I will force myself up and say, "It's time to get up and get going!"

WHAT ACTIVITY HAVE I found myself avoiding?

WHAT DISTRACTION ACTIVITY did I indulge in instead of the activity that really counts?

HOW CAN I remove these distractions or change my environment, so there are less temptations?

RHYME XXXVII
MOVE FORTH

RHYME 37

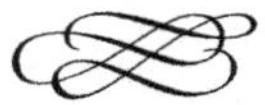

MOVE FORTH

You've made past choices and they've shaped who you are,

heed they not hold you from following your star.

MOVE FORTH

When moving forward with your plans, it is important to learn from your past experiences, but not let the negatives hold you back.

Consider the quote from the British novelist L.P. Hartley,

"The past is a foreign country; they do things differently there."

PREPARATION FOR USING RHYME 37

What thoughts, feelings or past experiences have a hold on me and consistently make me feel like I'm looking backwards rather than forwards?

WHAT THOUGHTS PROPEL ME FORWARD, is it running from the pain of the past, the pleasure of a future vision, or both? What is the pain? What is the hope?

WHAT EXACTLY ARE my guiding stars for the future?

PUTTING RHYME 37 INTO ACTION

When my thoughts drift to past events, I know my mind is unconsciously trying to protect me from possible future hurt, embarrassment, disappointment, and failure. This will keep me stuck in a comfortable state.

To break the state, I will ask:

- What is this thought trying to protect me from? What is its positive intention?
- How can I learn from this past experience to change and improve future experiences?

RHYME XXXVIII
FRESH CHANCE

RHYME 38

FRESH CHANCE

If past burdens you've collected weigh you down now,

---

drop them behind you, tread light on fresh ground.

FRESH CHANCE

By clinging to the past, you disempower your present. Never believe that a past memory is better than the moment you live in now,

---

as it has gone.

Flourish in this moment.

PREPARATION FOR USING RHYME 38

What ineffective, negative beliefs and physical possessions do I hold onto which I need to unburden myself from?

- Beliefs:
- Possessions:

WHAT PAST HOBBIES and dreams no longer hold their allure?

WHAT RELATIONSHIPS once important to me are now unsalvageable and do more harm than good?

PUTTING RHYME 38 INTO ACTION

I will choose a burden currently on my mind to work on today.

Does this (thought, belief, item, hobby, career or relationship) still serve me well in my daily life?

Is it worth saving or is it a lost cause and no longer brings satisfaction nor value?

Do I just enjoy the idea of it, am I stuck in my ways, or do I actually want to possess this or believe that?

RHYME XXXIX
ATTITUDE CONTROL

RHYME 39

ATTITUDE CONTROL

When you have little control of your situation,

---

changing your attitude is your one salvation.

ATTITUDE CONTROL

Our attitude is the only thing we can control in life.

Others, and our physical surroundings,

---

can only be influenced.

PREPARATION FOR USING RHYME 39

Knowing that only I can control my attitude in response to the events in my life, what attitudes do I have a preference for presenting to the world?

WHAT NEGATIVE ATTITUDES would I like to present less?

HOW MANY WAYS do I doubt the effectiveness of these negative attitudes and why must they go?

PUTTING RHYME 39 INTO ACTION

When I catch myself with a negative attitude, I will stop, bring myself into the moment with a focused deep breath, and re-frame it into a positive.

WHAT NEGATIVE ATTITUDE did I cast doubt upon today and what positive attitude can I re-frame it into?

- Negative:
- Positive:

RHYME XL
NOTHING IS NEW

RHYME 40

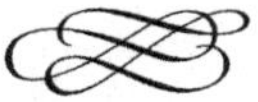

NOTHING IS NEW

All on earth will happen again as it has happened before,

---

nothing is new within our world of this you can be sure.

NOTHING IS NEW

Short-term memory causes us to forget that experiences may be new to us but not in human history.

You will have peace again, grief again, fun and boredom too.

Things will pass and occur again in one form or another.

PREPARATION FOR USING RHYME 40

Whenever I think that something is new or original, I will remind myself that it has happened before.

Everything is unoriginal; 'originality' comes from ideas being presented in a different form; a different combination of benefits and appearance. Sometimes, the level of passion or stylisation with which an idea is delivered, convinces us that it is new.

Is there an idea I haven't followed because I feel that it is unoriginal? What has held me back?

In what way am I passionate and/or have a different take on my idea compared to others?

PUTTING RHYME 40 INTO ACTION

Today I will make a conscious connection between 'new' products or approaches and those I have experienced in the past.

WHAT HAVE I NOTICED TODAY, presented as original, but is simply a re-hash of a re-hash?

WHAT IDEA CAUGHT my thoughts today that I could present in an 'original' way?

RHYME XLI
BE CAUTIOUS

RHYME 41

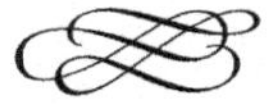

BE CAUTIOUS

If you play with snakes you will be bitten,

---

be aware of those who stay well-hidden.

BE CAUTIOUS

By putting yourself amidst the wrong crowd or befriending a less than scrupulous individual,

---

you invite danger upon yourself.

Be astute to those around you and expect the unexpected.

PREPARATION FOR USING RHYME 41

Who has led me on or turned on me when I least expected it?

Why do I think they did that?

How did it make me feel?

What signs do I need to be alert to in future relationships?

As I get to know new acquaintances properly, how can I maintain a level of caution and remain friendly?

PUTTING RHYME 41 INTO ACTION

People seek payoffs from others, either consciously or unconsciously, e.g. a sale, a commitment, reassurance and validation, control, power, gratification etc. Always question, "What's really in this for them?"

WHAT WARNING signs of insincerity did I notice today?

REFLECTING ON AN INTERACTION TODAY, "What was in it for them?"

HOW DID I respond to them and did I feel that I was could prevent myself from being manipulated?

RHYME XLII
BE VIGILANT

RHYME 42

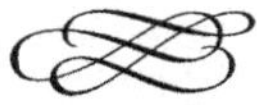

BE VIGILANT

Not everyone is your trusted friend,

---

a selfish friend craves a selfish end.

BE VIGILANT

Though we should always see the good in people, some will be self-seeking and serving.

Your friendships cannot be based on what you need from them,

---

nor can you be exploited by what others need from you.

PREPARATION FOR USING RHYME 42

How am I careful to not over-share personal information or feelings in less familiar relationships?

Do I feel that I am being used or dominated in any of my relationships?

Am I sustaining any relationships where I am certain I am being spoken of badly, behind my back?

PUTTING RHYME 42 INTO ACTION

To confront an unhealthy relationship, I can follow these steps:

- I won't overshare with people I don't fully know.
- I won't participate in controlling mind games, particularly lies to make me doubt my viewpoint.
- If they are demanding something from me, I will say I am busy and ignore their guilt tactics for not supporting them. A manipulator will take advantage of my weaknesses and try and wear me down.
- I will let the relationship fade with less and less contact and socialise with other friends instead.
- I will seek professional support if they become threatening or dangerous.

WHAT ACTIONS WILL I start today to address an unhealthy and undesirable relationship?

RHYME XLIII
ALWAYS ASTUTE

RHYME 43

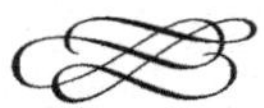

ALWAYS ASTUTE

Don't always believe all that you hear,

---

if it's too good to be true, it's best to steer clear.

ALWAYS ASTUTE

As most things do not come easily,

---

promises of ‘easy’ are probably false,

---

especially from an over-sharing stranger.

PREPARATION FOR USING RHYME 43

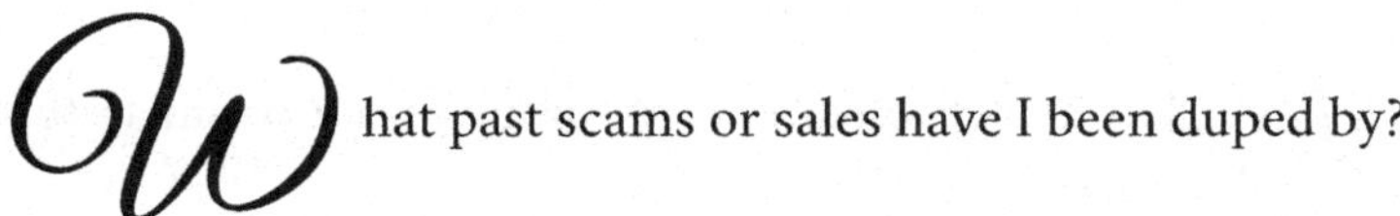

What past scams or sales have I been duped by?

What did I lose as a result and how did I feel after it happened?

What was it about me that they took advantage of?

Being too polite, kind, good-natured, friendly, helpful, or avoiding an awkward feeling?

What would I have done differently in hindsight?

PUTTING RHYME 43 INTO ACTION

When I consider spending my money on a promise for something better, I will ask,
"Is this too good to be true?"

WHAT PROMISES HAVE I come across today that caught my attention? What sales method was used to convince me? i.e. To improve appearance; have better success in life, love and career; streamline; save time; save money; increase status; or transcend the mundane.

HOW ELSE COULD I achieve these promises without spending?

RHYME XLIV
PRAISE OTHERS

RHYME 44

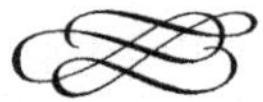

PRAISE OTHERS

Say to them "You have..." before you compliment,

---

say it sincerely and with good intent.

PRAISE OTHERS

By praising someone's abilities or traits by using the "You have..." phrase, such as

"You have a great way of making people feel at ease,"

you intentionally and personably raise their esteem.

PREPARATION FOR USING RHYME 44

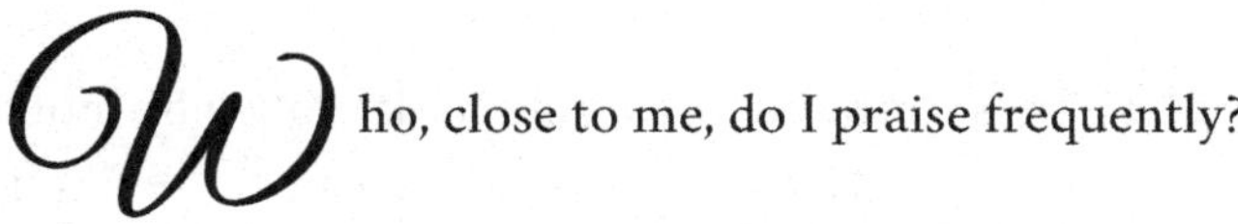

Who, close to me, do I praise frequently?

WHAT DO I praise them for and with what intent?

WHO, close to me, I do not praise enough?

WHY DO I not feel they need praise from me?

WHAT REALISTIC AND positive praise could I plan to gift them, in an appropriate and timely way, acknowledging their importance to me?

PUTTING RHYME 44 INTO ACTION

Do I validate those around me enough? If not, why not? Today, I will praise at least one person using the "You have…" phrase.

- You have a great sense of…
- You have a natural ability to…
- You have good promise in…
- You have a wonderful way of…

I will keep my praise relevant, sincere, and not over-the-top.

Who did I praise today and did they react positively?

Do I need to re-think the way I give praise, ready for tomorrow?

RHYME XLV
HONEST COMMUNICATION

RHYME 45

HONEST COMMUNICATION

If you're not happy with someone's behaviour,

---

say, "I've a problem with this, please do me the favour..."

HONEST COMMUNICATION

If you are affected by somebody else's behaviour, if they don't know, they'll likely repeat it without the chance to correct it,

---

for example, kindly say,

"Hi . . ., just so you know for next time, I have a problem with the nickname you call me. Please do me the favour of saying my name correctly."

PREPARATION FOR USING RHYME 45

In which situations am I not assertive when people behave in a way towards me that I don't find acceptable?

WHAT STOPS me from expressing how I feel?

WHEN AND HOW could I feel comfortable using this statement? "I've a problem with ..., please do me the favour..."

PUTTING RHYME 45 INTO ACTION

Today, I will speak up if the behaviour of another affects me in an unacceptable way and say,
"I've a problem with …, please do me the favour…".
Delivering it kindly and politely.

Do I need to modify the statement to suit my manner?

Did anyone's behaviour affect me personally today?

Why did I feel so impacted by their behaviour?

What was their response to my assertive approach with them?

RHYME XLVI
ASK PERMISSION

RHYME 46

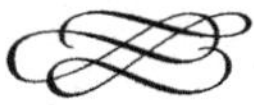

ASK PERMISSION

Never demand others to do something for you,

instead ask for consent "Would you be willing to...?"

ASK PERMISSION

Other people are not your inferiors at your beck and call.

Nothing should happen to someone for your personal gain,

---

without their willingness to participate.

PREPARATION FOR USING RHYME 46

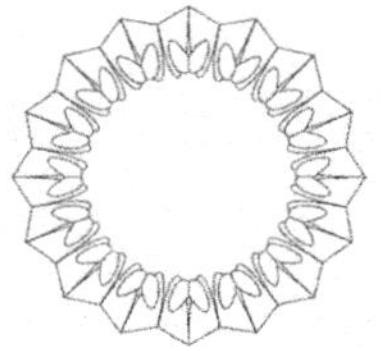

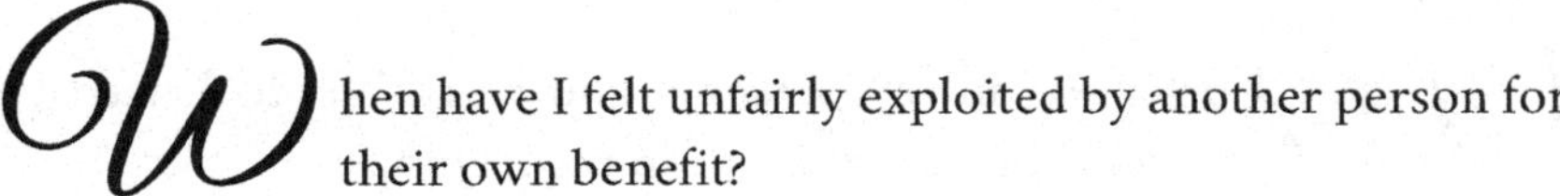

When have I felt unfairly exploited by another person for their own benefit?

When have I made unfair demands of others without their agreement?

In what instances from my day-to-day life can I imagine needing to ask consent from someone so that I am not consciously exploiting them?

PUTTING RHYME 46 INTO ACTION

What areas in my personal and work life do I need to start asking for consent, starting with, "Would you be willing to...?"

After trying the phrase today when I needed another's consent, what happened and how did they respond?

Do I need to adjust my approach when asking for consent? What would better suited my manner?

RHYME XLVII
PLAN BACKWARDS

RHYME 47

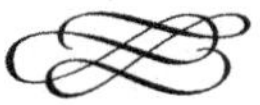

PLAN BACKWARDS

Start with the outcome,

---

mark each step back one.

PLAN BACKWARDS

Visualise your desired end point.

Step backwards through the process of getting there, all the way to the beginning.

Account for each predicted realistic action and possible pitfall.

PREPARATION FOR USING RHYME 47

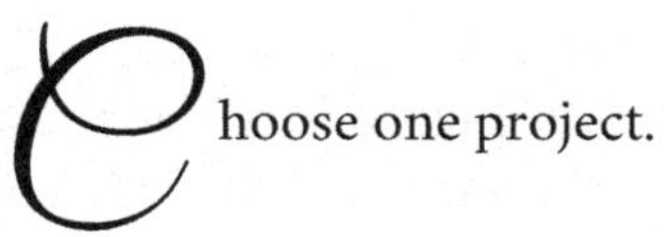

Choose one project.

How do I visualise the outcome of my project?

What action would I need to achieve one step before this outcome?

Outline each preceding action step, back to the very first action.

Take the first action now.

PUTTING RHYME 47 INTO ACTION

I will make it a practice to plan from the desired outcome back to the very first action, accounting for any foreseen pitfalls along the way and how I might deal with these challenges as they arise.

I will then take on the very first action immediately.

WHAT ARE the actions I am taking today?

DID I need to make any adjustments to these actions?

DID any tricky obstacles come up that I needed to address?

RHYME XLVIII
ONLY NOW

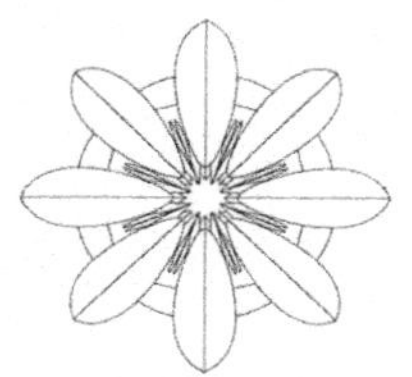

RHYME 48

ONLY NOW

If you think of each day as if it's your last,

---

you'll live in the moment and not in the past.

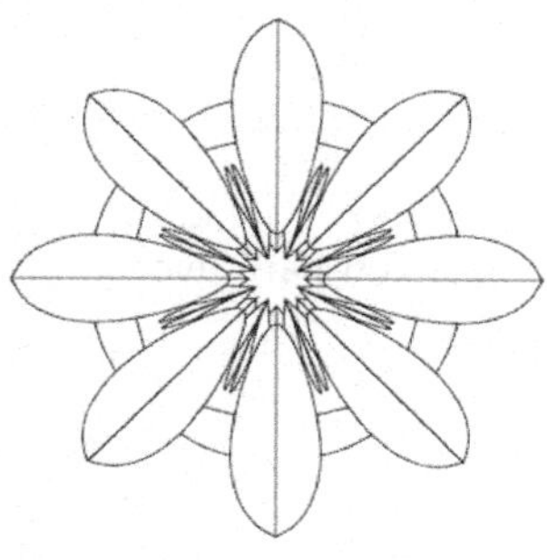

ONLY NOW

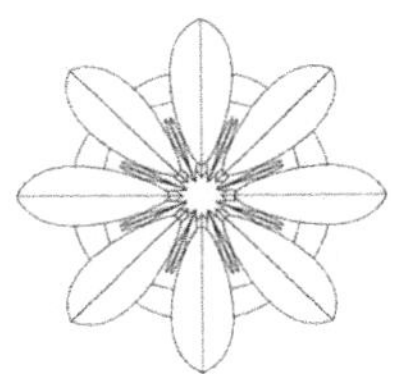

A favourite philosophical technique of the ancient Greek stoics was to ponder death and put their life now into an appreciated perspective.

The stoic Roman Emperor Marcus Aurelius said,

"Think of yourself as dead. You have lived your life. Now take what's left and live it properly."

PREPARATION FOR USING RHYME 48

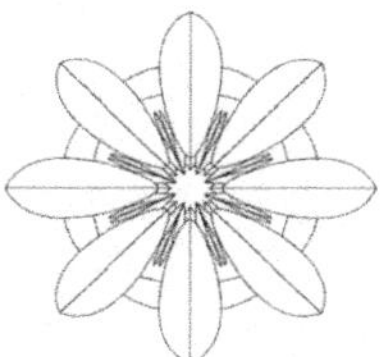

Life is unpredictable. I must do whatever it takes to live well whilst I can, in my way, not someone else's.

Do I live each day in respect of having been given the chance of life for another day?

Do I focus daily on the things I am grateful for?

Can I make it a habit to reflect with gratitude on the small pleasures and wonders I encounter throughout the day?

i.e. A gratitude journal, giving thanks for simple pleasures, bringing myself into the moment, the opportunity to enhance another's life, savouring things rather than rushing them without appreciation etc.

PUTTING RHYME 48 INTO ACTION

Eventually you will come to know that life passes quickly. Learn to savour and appreciate the small things.

TODAY, I will catch myself in a moment and ask, "Am I savouring this experience or rushing it?"

ON WAKING, I will ask "What three things am I looking forward to today?"

ON GOING TO BED, I will ask myself, "What three things am I grateful for happening today?"

RHYME XLIX
BE GRATEFUL

RHYME 49

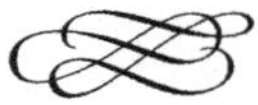

BE GRATEFUL

The grass is always greener on the other side of the fence,

---

but jealousy and envy will make your life tense.

BE GRATEFUL

Jealousy is insecurity, the feeling of your life being in-equal compared to others.

Be grateful for what you have rather than what you lack,

---

you can be certain that someone else envies your lot in life.

PREPARATION FOR USING RHYME 49

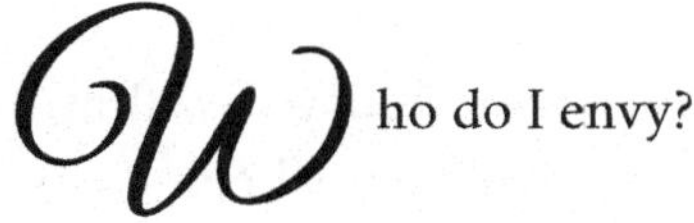ho do I envy?

WHAT DO they possess that I feel I lack?

WHAT FEELING MIGHT I experience if I possessed what they had?

CAN I have that same feeling now through similar or other ways?

PUTTING RHYME 49 INTO ACTION

When I find myself envious of others today, I will ask, "What is the feeling I actually want that is behind this envy?"

COMMENT ON THE FOLLOWING:

- Does possessing something guarantee I will no longer be envious ever again? Why/Why not?
- Does having a certain relationship guarantee I will no longer be envious ever again? Why/Why not?
- Does having a certain title, social position or career guarantee I will no longer be envious again? Why/Why not?

WHAT AM I so insecure about?

RHYME L
NO BLAME

RHYME 50

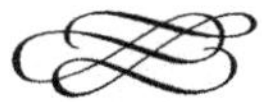

NO BLAME

When you criticise, condemn or complain,

---

you scar your relationship through hurtful blame.

NO BLAME

When you declare that someone or something is to blame for a fault or wrong against you or the world, you disempower your life through irresponsibility.

It takes an enlightened person to allow another a chance for redemption,

---

through forgiveness.

PREPARATION FOR USING RHYME 50

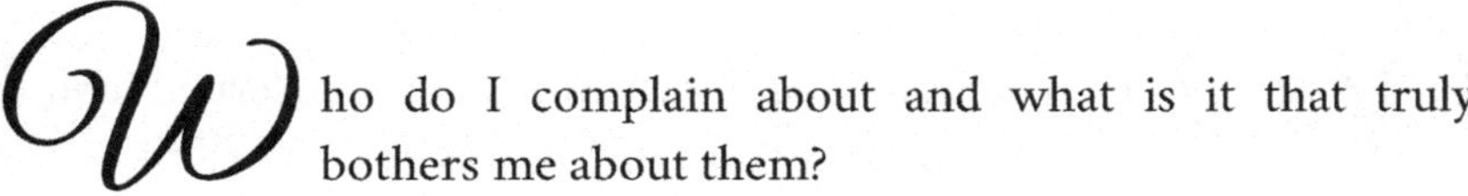

Who do I complain about and what is it that truly bothers me about them?

WHAT FLAW of my owning is this a reflection of, and what do I need to work on?

HOW CAN I respond responsibly to people and their behaviours that raise my anxiety?

PUTTING RHYME 50 INTO ACTION

When frustrated, angry, anxious, or concerned about another person, I will:

1. bite my tongue and hold back my first response
2. take a deep breath to calm my emotions
3. wait to respond from an empowered position

There needs to be a benefit to the person to who I am responding,

e.g. "I've a problem with how your projects are not completed by deadlines, would you consider sharing a schedule to meet them that I can support you with?"

WHAT RESPONSES CAN I draft up for situations I may face today?

RHYME LI

YOU ALONE

RHYME 51

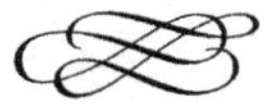

ONLY YOU

Unto thine own self be true,

---

they are them, but you are you.

YOU ALONE

You must live your own life.

You cannot be someone else,

---

no matter how much you admire, envy or imitate them.

PREPARATION FOR USING RHYME 51

In what ways am I being true to myself; the actions, behaviours and beliefs that I embody?

In what ways am I not being true to myself; the actions, behaviours and beliefs of others that I am imitating or being ruled by?

In what ways do I act like someone I am not?

For whom do I behave this way?

PUTTING RHYME 51 INTO ACTION

If I feel tempted to act in ways that are simply not true to myself, I will say,

"To thine own self be true."

WHAT UNCOMFORTABLE 'NOT TRUE TO ME' behaviours will I avoid today?

WHAT BEHAVIOURS DID I exhibit today that aligned with being myself?

RHYME LII
COST OF CHOICE

RHYME 52

COST OF CHOICE

Where there is a will there is a way,

---

and a price that you'll have to pay.

COST OF CHOICE

Every action costs, whether that cost be in time, health, relationships or money.

Accepting that some price will be paid,

---

you can pursue your goal vigorously.

PREPARATION FOR USING RHYME 52

List the choices currently occupying my mind, whether for physical goods, personal change, social status, career, health and fitness:

1. Current Desire:
2. Actual Cost:
3. Benefit:
4. Does the benefit outweigh the cost?

1. gym membership
2. monthly fee of……. and two hours per day, three to five days per week.
3. Health and fitness, well-being, stress relief.
4. My fitness and well-being are a priority and the cost and time are a small price for my health.

WHICH OF MY desires are realistically unaffordable at this moment?

PUTTING RHYME 52 INTO ACTION

Today when I am making a choice, I will ask:

"Does the actual cost outweigh the benefit of this choice?"

I will be realistic about the cost of my choice.

In what situation today did I weigh up the benefits versus the actual cost?

What happened today when I had a choice but did nothing?

What was the actual cost of doing nothing?

RHYME LIII
EXPECT CONSEQUENCES

RHYME 53

EXPECT CONSEQUENCES

Whether you do or you don't, whether you will, or you won't,

---

a path you will follow with an end result.

EXPECT CONSEQUENCES

For every action or inaction, positive or negative,

there will be a consequence,

positive or negative.

PREPARATION FOR USING RHYME 53

There are consequences for all that I do. Consequences are simply cause and effect, expected or unexpected. What counts is how I constructively make use of them.

KNOWING that there will always be a consequence, what can I predict will happen from experience for an action I will be taking soon?

HAVE I thought through and prepared myself for the possible consequences of this action? How?

1. My Action:
2. The Expected Outcome:
3. My Preparation:

PUTTING RHYME 53 INTO ACTION

I will think in terms of:

"The balance of probabilities";

that is, the likelihood that something will happen in ways similar to past experiences.

- Before I take this action, what is the balance of probabilities that the outcome will be favourable?
- Did the outcome occur similarly to how I expected? In what way?
- Did I underestimate or overestimate the actual result of the outcome in terms of its timeframe or cost?

RHYME LIV
SELF-APPROVAL

RHYME 54

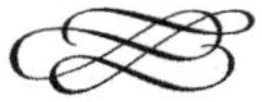

SELF-APPROVAL

You can't please everyone,

---

so, wish them well and just please some.

SELF-APPROVAL

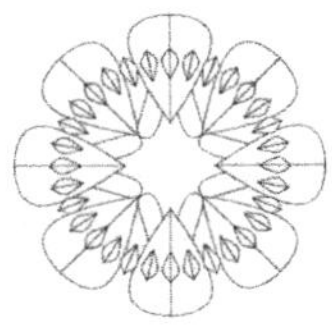

You will fail to please everyone as someone will always be dissatisfied.

People's differences in values and expectations make it very difficult to gain everyone's approval,

---

so simply don't expect to.

PREPARATION FOR USING RHYME 54

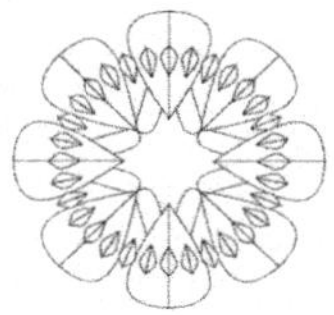

What feelings do I get by gaining the approval of another?

How do I feel if someone disapproves or I think that they do?

What lengths and sacrifices do I go to, to get another's approval?

Why is it unhealthy for me to seek approval?

What do I need to believe or do to stop seeking approval?

PUTTING RHYME 54 INTO ACTION

Today, when I am wanting the approval of others, I will choose one of the following phrases that rings true for me and say it to myself:

- "I am good enough" or "I only need my approval."
- "I am doing this from my best intentions."
- "Does it really matter what this person thinks?"
- "Why is it so important what they think?"
- "Who cares what they think, my thoughts are valid."

WHAT MOMENTS HAVE I sought approval today or had thoughts of desiring another's approval?

WHAT DID I SAY, or could I have said, to reaffirm my own self-approval?

RHYME LV
INEVITABLE IMPERMANENCE

RHYME 55

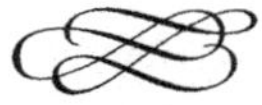

INEVITABLE IMPERMANENCE

What excites you won't last,

---

what drains you will pass.

INEVITABLE IMPERMANENCE

Excitement is brief and short-lived,

---

so too are the troubles we face in life,

---

and our life itself.

PREPARATION FOR USING RHYME 55

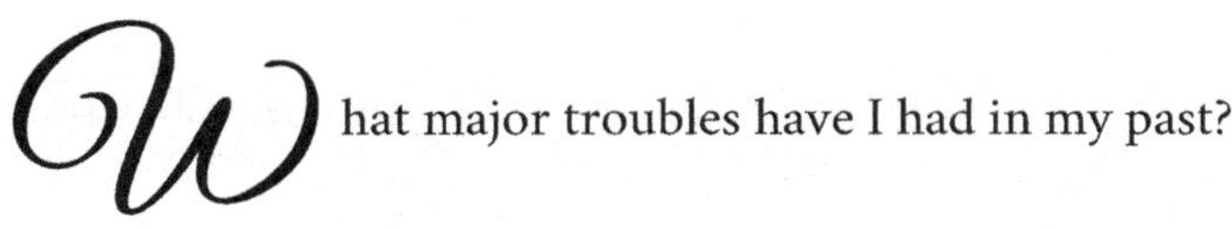

What major troubles have I had in my past?

How did they come to pass in the end?

What troubles do I have at the moment?

How can I influence them to come to pass?

What specifically can I do to enjoy this moment now, in-between the problems I may be facing?

PUTTING RHYME 55 INTO ACTION

When faced with a problem today, I will remember that it will pass and take a proactive approach:

- Do I have any control over this problem or is there a way to influence it for the better?
- What can I do to confront this problem, avoid it for now, or make it more bearable?
- What can I do better to raise my strength and resilience, my way of thinking about and handling this problem?
- Am I finding this problem too difficult and need help from a trusted friend or an appropriate professional?

RHYME LVI
OPINIONS - PREFERENCES

RHYME 56

OPINIONS - PREFERENCES

There's no point carrying that chip on your shoulder,

---

when you know beauty sits in the eye of the beholder.

OPINIONS - PREFERENCES

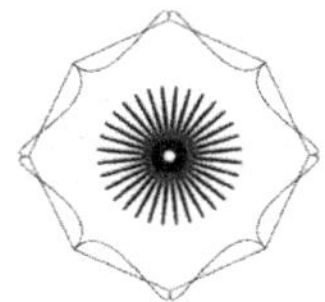

In older times, one would place a wooden chip on their shoulder daring any who disagreed with their argument to knock it off, resulting in a fight.

We all have differing views of the world, placing our own value on what is important to us.

All good opinions are backed by factual evidence, and preferences simply a personal choice.

PREPARATION FOR USING RHYME 56

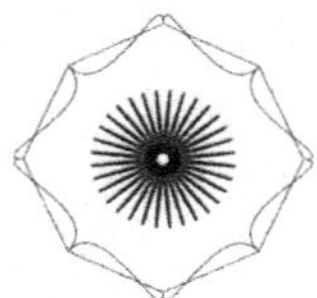

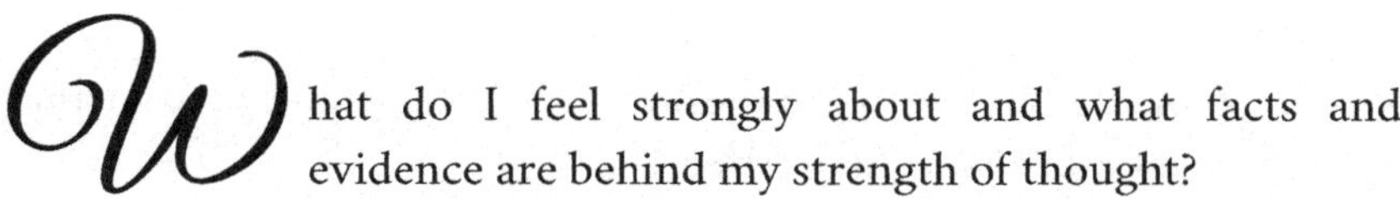

What do I feel strongly about and what facts and evidence are behind my strength of thought?

WHAT BELIEFS or lifestyle of others, raise my emotions?

KNOWING that I can only influence another, what factual approach would I take, without expecting them to agree?

WHAT PREFERENCES DO I HAVE?

WHAT THOUGHTS and experiences are behind my preferences?

PUTTING RHYME 56 INTO ACTION

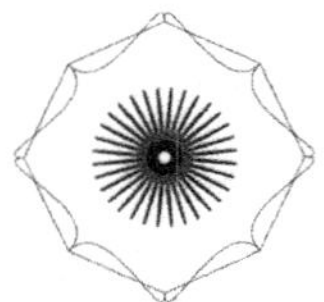

Today I will separate opinions from facts and respect that another's view may differ. I can say:

- "I'm interested in your view and listening to the evidence behind it."
- "What facts have led you to this opinion?"
- "My view differs from the fact that..."

WHAT OPINIONS DID I encounter today?

WHICH OPINIONS DIFFERED FROM MINE?

WHAT PREFERENCES DID I seek today and what reason was behind my choice?

RHYME LVII
OWN YOUR CRITICISM

RHYME 57

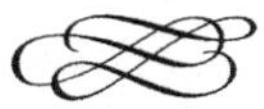

OWN YOUR CRITICISM

If you blame others for your discontent,

---

you're being servile, passive and co-dependent.

OWN YOUR CRITICISM

Criticism is finding fault in a disapproving way.

By belittling and trying to control others,

---

you reveal your insecurity.

PREPARATION FOR USING RHYME 57

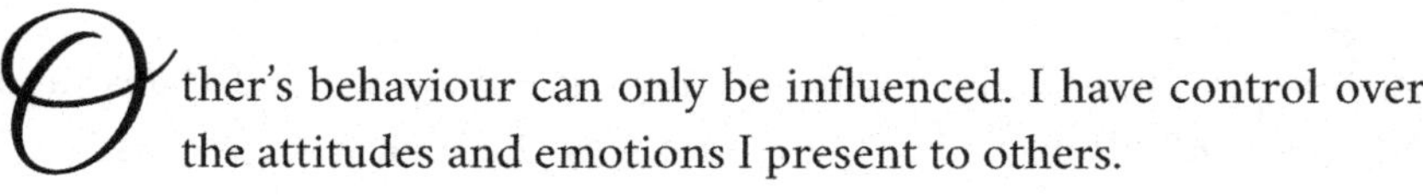

Other's behaviour can only be influenced. I have control over the attitudes and emotions I present to others.

WHAT NEGATIVE ATTITUDES have I dumped on another?

WHICH OF MY negative emotions are triggered easily by others and what are the triggers?

HOW CAN I catch myself being negative with others?

WHAT DO I need to do to stop my negativity towards others?

PUTTING RHYME 57 INTO ACTION

Today I will begin owning my negative attitudes and emotions rather than projecting them on someone else.

I will use whatever technique I can to prevent expressing my first impulsive reaction when someone frustrates or angers me. I could:

- bite my tongue
- take a deep breath and hold it for a moment
- squeeze my thumb and a finger together
- ask to discuss it later and set up an immediate time, when I don't feel like I am on the back foot

---

WHAT OTHER STRATEGIES might work best for me today?

WHAT STRATEGIES DID I actually use today?

RHYME LVIII
GET ON

RHYME 58

GET ON

To put off 'til tomorrow, next week or someday,

---

is no troubling thought when you act today.

GET ON

We tie ourselves in knots by choosing rapid-reward, short-term pleasures over taking steps toward time-consuming, but beneficial, long-term accomplishments.

We need to raise the value of our long-term desires by recognising that,

---

short-term pleasures consume our valuable time.

PREPARATION FOR USING RHYME 58

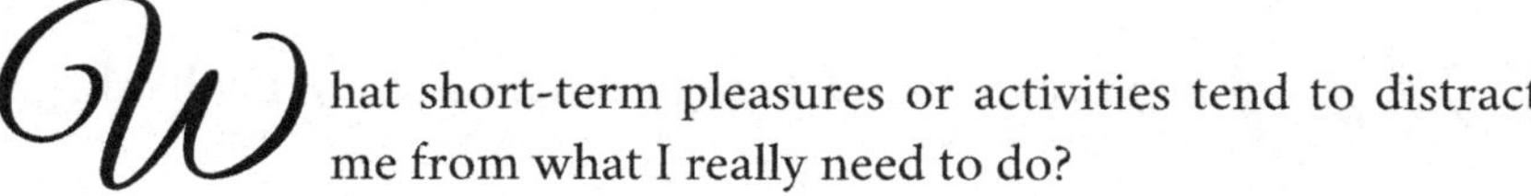

What short-term pleasures or activities tend to distract me from what I really need to do?

How can I develop my discipline for putting long-term goals first?

i.e. scheduling/timetabling long-term actions and sticking to them, hiding or removing short/term distractions or even locking them away.

What short-term pleasures can I use as rewards after I've been working on long-term activities for an adequate time?

PUTTING RHYME 58 INTO ACTION

When I catch myself being distracted today, I will ask: What is the cost of this short-term pleasure on my long-term accomplishment?

WHAT IMPORTANT LONG-TERM projects have I put off today or not worked on sufficiently?

WHAT SHORT-TERM PLEASURES distracted me from these tasks?

HOW WILL I remove the distraction for tomorrow?

RHYME LIX
CARELESS TALK

RHYME 59

CARELESS TALK

If you can't say anything nice, don't say anything at all,

---

there's no grace nor compassion making others feel small.

CARELESS TALK

Sometimes to preserve the health of your relationships with others, you must keep your thoughts to yourself.

The Philosopher Jean-Paul Sartre said,

"Words are loaded pistols."

PREPARATION FOR USING RHYME 59

Think of a recent time when I used negative words intending to get a certain response from another person.

WHAT NEGATIVE WORDS did I use to hurt, anger, or provoke them into a reaction or emotion?

WHAT WAS my intention and how did I feel about doing it?

HOW COULD I have better influenced them in a positive way?

PUTTING RHYME 59 INTO ACTION

Today, if I need to influence another to do something, rather than manipulate them, I will be straight and tell the truth:

- "This is the situation as I see it…"
- "I feel strongly…"
- "I'd like to suggest we do the following…"
- "These are how I see the facts…"
- "From my viewpoint…"
- "I respect you and I want to be direct…"
- "Let me tell you how I observed it…"
- "I understand that…"

---

1. When today have I been more straightforward?
2. How did I feel about being more straightforward?
3. How did the person/people react?
4. How do I need to improve my straightforward approach?

RHYME LX
TEMPORARY OWNERSHIP

RHYME 60

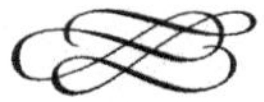

TEMPORARY OWNERSHIP

Most stuff rusts,

---

or turns to dust.

TEMPORARY OWNERSHIP

That shiny, new treasure you covet will grow old,

---

be replaced, be lost, be stolen or become junk,

---

eventually.

PREPARATION FOR USING RHYME 60

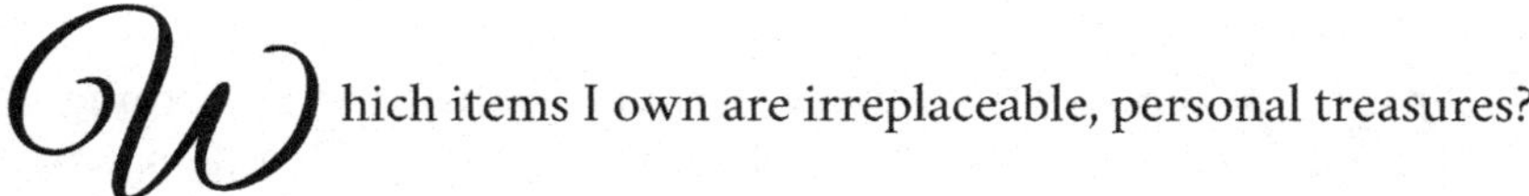

hich items I own are irreplaceable, personal treasures?

How would I feel if I got rid of less important items?

What have I felt guilty for buying recently?

Am I quick to replace gadgets with the latest update? Why?

Every time I do buy something, I will follow the rule, “One thing in, one thing out!” (or more out if I’m serious!)

PUTTING RHYME 60 INTO ACTION

When faced with the compulsion to buy something, I will remember that after I have bought it, I may experience 'buyer's remorse' for having spent money on it. I will likely soon lose the 'buyer's high' of the purchase and probably look towards my next hunt.

CHOOSE A CURRENTLY DESIRED item and ask:

1. Would this serve a valuable purpose? What exactly does it promise to deliver?
2. Will I still appreciate owning this in a year and is it worth the cost?
3. What would happen if I didn't buy it, could I be more resourceful instead and better use what I already have? How?

RHYME LXI
REIGN IN IMPULSIVENESS

RHYME 61

REIGN IN IMPULSIVENESS

When your thoughts and behaviours are running wild,

---

who's in charge, your adult or child?

REIGN IN IMPULSIVENESS

People can be mature and deliberate, or immature and impulsive at any age.

Mature people show others respect, are genuine, accept personal responsibility, and

---

are the bigger person in the face of another's immaturity and impulsiveness.

PREPARATION FOR USING RHYME 61

Immature actions are often conducted at the expense of others.

What impulsive things do I do that impact on those around me?

What feeling am I trying to accomplish through these impulsive actions?

Are there better ways I can get these feelings?

PUTTING RHYME 61 INTO ACTION

Today, if I am tempted by an immature, impulsive action that will negatively cost me or someone else, I will ask:

- "What feeling am I trying to achieve from this?"
- "How else can I get the same feeling more deliberately?"
- "Am I just irresponsibly escaping from a feeling I don't like?"
- "What irresponsible behaviours have I indulged in today?"
- "How did I feel after indulging in them?"
- "Was it worth the cost and is it sustainable without myself or anyone else being affected?"

RHYME LXII
SHOW RESILIENCE

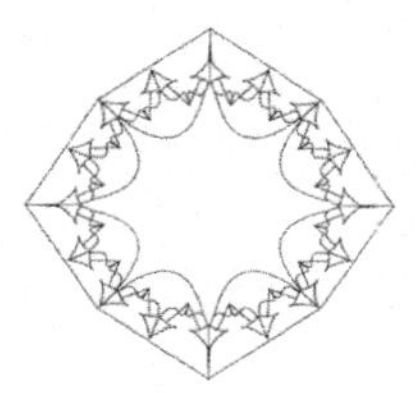

RHYME 62

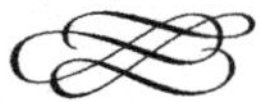

SHOW RESILIENCE

When you think you've travelled and exhausted all trails,

---

there are more to discover and an answer prevails.

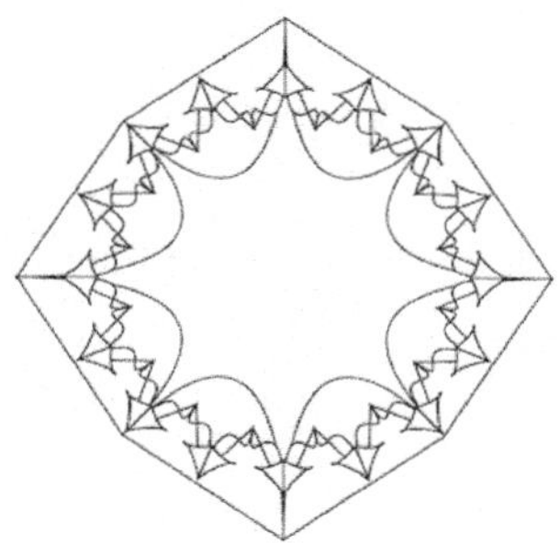

SHOW RESILIENCE

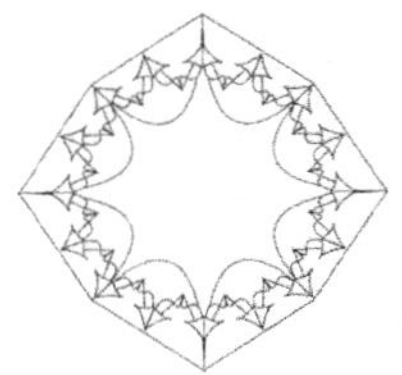

Your ability to recover quickly from difficulties is a mark of your resilience.

Challenge your feelings of doubt and

---

believe in your natural ability to adapt.

PREPARATION FOR USING RHYME 62

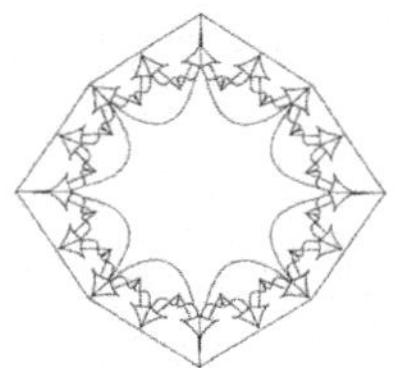

In many of life's situations, if one person can manage something, it is pretty likely that I can learn to do the same.

WHAT DO I doubt that I can handle in life?

WHAT EXPERIENCE CAN I draw upon from my past where I have overcome a difficult situation? What did I do?

WHAT INNER STRENGTH do I need to draw upon now to overcome this doubt and create an unwavering belief that I can do it?

PUTTING RHYME 62 INTO ACTION

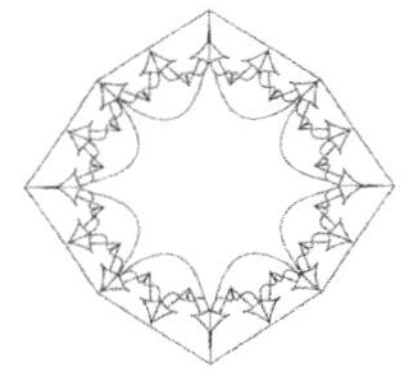

Doubt has not proven itself true yet, I will take strength in my ability to have a go and learn from my mistakes. Instead of doubt, I will believe that:

- "I can do it!"
- "I can find a way and I will learn from any mistakes."

WHAT HAVE I doubted about myself today?

WHAT WOULD it take to prove these doubts wrong?

WHAT ACTION AM I going to take to show that I believe in myself and these doubts are powerless?

RHYME LXIII
REDUCE IT

RHYME 63

REDUCE IT

Why work so hard to make ends meet,

---

have fewer ends which you have to complete.

REDUCE IT

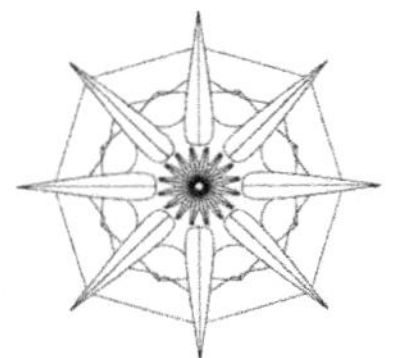

By overcommitting to too many projects, you are sacrificing quality for quantity, increasing your load and fraying your composure.

Instead, reduce things down to

---

the worthwhile experiences of life.

PREPARATION FOR USING RHYME 63

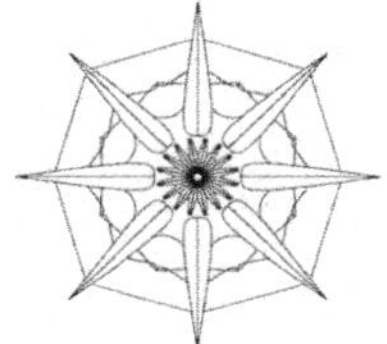

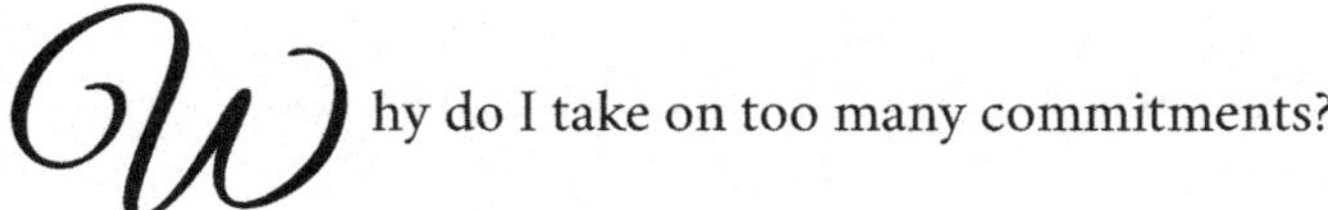

Why do I take on too many commitments?

Do I have a problem saying "No" to others when they ask me to take on another task?

What do I really want to focus on?

What physical, mental, hobby, and work-related commitments do I need to reduce to keep me from being overwhelmed?

PUTTING RHYME 63 INTO ACTION

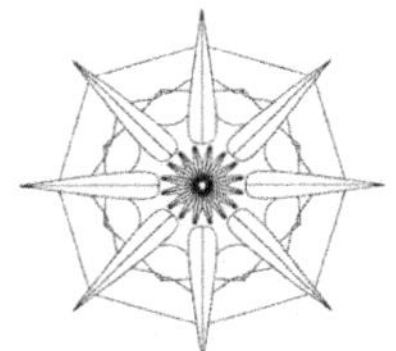

Today I will begin to say "No" to extraneous tasks.

- "Unfortunately I can't take this on until I have tied up other unfinished tasks. No guarantees, but I will let you know when I have the time."
- "I appreciate your urgency, but I don't have the time at the moment. Can I suggest..."

What have I said "No" to today?

Has it left me with space to get on with other priorities?

What further self-belief do I need to be able to say "No" to extra demands? What am I worried about if I say "No"?

RHYME LXIV
BRIEF EXCITEMENT

RHYME 64

BRIEF EXCITEMENT

Forever confusing excitement for passion,

is a short-lived venture and tiresome pattern.

BRIEF EXCITEMENT

Excitement burns like the brief flame of a match,

---

whereas passion simmers,

---

like the long-lasting coals of a fire.

PREPARATION FOR USING RHYME 64

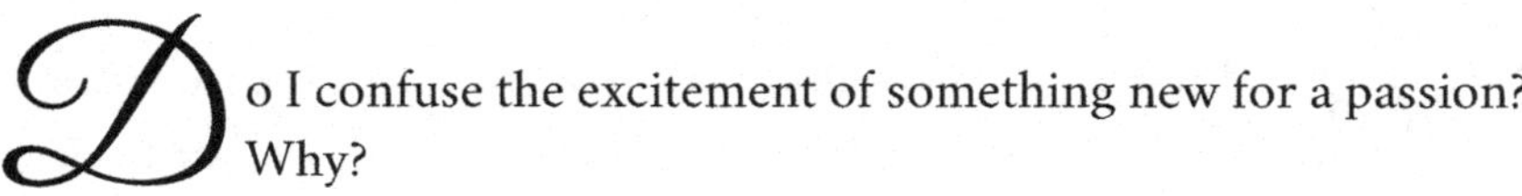

Do I confuse the excitement of something new for a passion? Why?

WHAT PROJECTS HAVE I got all excited about, and then as the excitement waned, given up on?

WHAT LONG SIMMERING passion do I truly think I should be doing for the long term?

WHY HAVEN'T I STARTED, or if I have, continued this project?

PUTTING RHYME 64 INTO ACTION

When I feel the sudden intensity to take something up, I will proceed carefully before spending time or money until I have done my research and I am sure.

Do I really think this new project will turn into something I want to spend time and money on?

Is this project just another fantasy self I would like to be that is not actually who I am?

Is THERE an authentic project that has been burning in the back of my mind that I must take up, resume or finish or I will regret it later?

RHYME LXV
STEP OUT

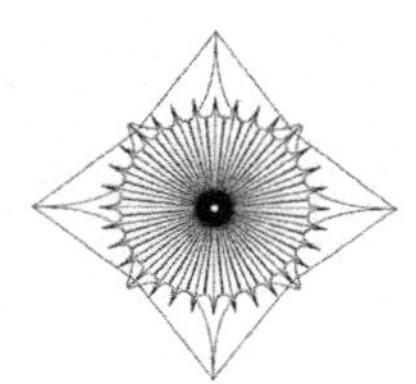

RHYME 65

STEP OUT

Life is too short to live in the shadows,

step out from the dark into life's sunny meadows.

STEP OUT

By simply being alive you have the chance to pursue your interests and not hide them away.

There's no need to compete or compare if you don't wish to,

---

though you never know, you might achieve more than you expected!

PREPARATION FOR USING RHYME 65

Am I living in the shadows? Who's shadow?

WHAT AM I AFRAID OF?

WHY ARE their interests more important than mine?

IF I DESIRED IT, what would I personally need to believe or do to step out and achieve more?

PUTTING RHYME 65 INTO ACTION

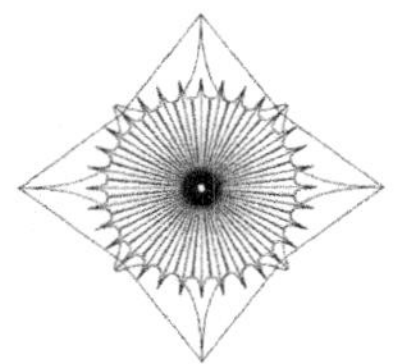

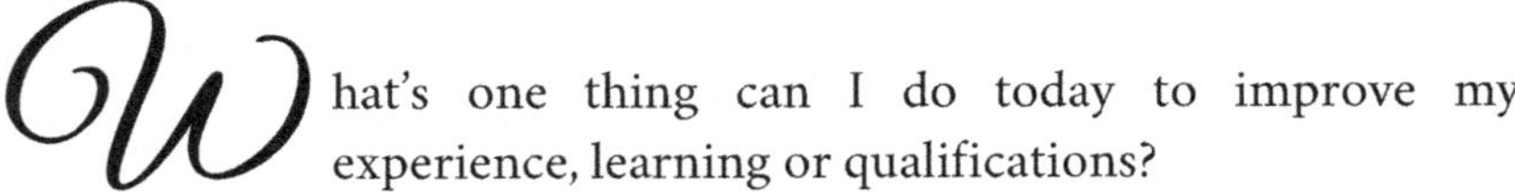

What's one thing can I do today to improve my experience, learning or qualifications?

What can I do today to raise my presence or positive impact?

On reflection, what will it take each day to achieve a higher level of understanding or performance in my area of interest?

RHYME LXVI
CHANGING SEASONS

RHYME 66

CHANGING SEASONS

All things in time must come to pass,

---

this isn't the first time and won't be the last.

CHANGING SEASONS

We have seasons in our lives

---

and they all come to an end.

Enjoy each season whilst you can.

PREPARATION FOR USING RHYME 66

There are seasons in our lives:

- In Spring we live our childhood and teen years.
- In Summer we live our twenties through thirties.
- In Autumn or Fall we live our forties through sixties.
- In Winter we live our seventies onward.

WHAT SEASON AM I IN, and what do I wish to achieve within it?

WHAT WOULD I like to change in this season?

WHAT AM I enjoying about this season whilst it lasts?

PUTTING RHYME 66 INTO ACTION

Everything has a shelf life with a 'best before' date. Don't waste it.

KNOWING the season I am in, what would I like to pursue today?

STARTING TODAY, what would I no longer like to put up and what can I do about it?

HAVE I taken a moment today to savour this time of my life?

RHYME LXVII
GRASP CHANCES

RHYME 67

GRASP CHANCES

What doesn't kill you makes you grow stronger,

---

don't miss opportunities through idle squander.

GRASP CHANCES

Embrace the chances you have now,

---

no matter how small.

Don't sit back and let chances drift by until it is too late.

PREPARATION FOR USING RHYME 67

We have to take certain risks in order to grow our experience and learning.

WHAT RISKS or opportunities have I been presented with recently?

IF I FOLLOWED ONE THROUGH, what happened?

HOW DID that make me feel?

CAN I foresee any chances for risk or opportunity coming up?

PUTTING RHYME 67 INTO ACTION

Today I will seek opportunities that involve slightly uncomfortable risks, whether the risk is real or just imagined.

I will say to myself,

"Whatever happens, I can see it through!"

WHAT SMALL RISKS or opportunities presented themselves today?

DID I miss an opportunity today that I regret not taking?

RHYME LXVIII
STEP-BY-STEP

RHYME 68

STEP-BY-STEP

Few things come easily and take toil and time,

---

secure each step up the hill that you climb.

STEP-BY-STEP

Live in this moment, and take things in your stride,

---

step-by-step and never say die.

Don't squander your energy on past and future times.

PREPARATION FOR USING RHYME 68

Everything I do and every step I take is a process to achieve a feeling.

A feeling is ultimately fleeting and eventually just an impression left in my memory.

Some may hike up Mount Everest to attain a feeling of awe, others may meditate each day in a quiet space to achieve a feeling of awe. There are many paths to the same feeling.

WHAT DO I want to feel more of?

WHAT EFFORT WILL IT TAKE?

WHAT CAN I say when the going gets tough? maybe "The tough get going!" or "The tough get rough!"?

PUTTING RHYME 68 INTO ACTION

Today, what step do I need to take toward what I want?

Is my step realistically achievable and the risks not too high?

How will I know when I have achieved this step? What will I feel?

How can I reward myself appropriately once I have achieved this step toward my goal?

RHYME LXIX

I

RHYME 69

I

In life, it's not what I do, get or see,

---

all that counts is feeling good about me.

ABOUT THE AUTHOR

A-J Paterson resides in London, England, and works in school management consultancy and is an author of books and articles on school leadership and personal self-development. A-J has taught in and led a number of Government and Private schools and holds a UK National Professional Qualification for Headteachers, Advanced Skills Teaching certification, a B.Ed. (Hons.) and Post-Grad in Business Management.

With so many complicated and often confusing school curriculums, A-J is driven to teach minimal, highly engaging and experiential lessons, resulting in a learner's higher retainment and attainment, and love for learning.

After studying at the London School of Clinical Hypnosis and then Neuro-Linguistic Programming with Richard Bandler and Paul McKenna, A-J developed a passion for using language to help others change their lives.

You can find out more by visiting:

miniteaching.com

Made in United States
Orlando, FL
20 December 2021